Solving the College Admissions Puzzle

A Guide for Students and Families About College Selection, Essay Writing, and High-Stakes Testing

John B. Boshoven, MA, MSW, LPC,
Debbie E. Merion, MFA, MSW, and
Geraldine Markel, PhD

©2016 by John Boshoven, Debbie Merion & Geraldine Markel

2016 Edition
Solving the College Admissions Puzzle: A Guide for Students and Families About College Selection, Essay Writing, and High-Stakes Testing ©2016
by John Boshoven, Debbie Merion & Geraldine Markel
Layout and updated design: Lana Campbell
Printed in the United States of America
Print ISBN: 978-0-9971762-0-9
Kindle ISBN: for Kindle: 978-0-9971762-1-6

Published by Managing Your Mind, LLC.
Ann Arbor, MI
www.managingyourmind.com
Telephone/Fax: 734 761 6498

2011 Edition
Solving the College Admissions Puzzle: A Guide for Students and Families About College Selection, Essay Writing, and High-Stakes Testing ©2011 by John Boshoven, Debbie Merion & Geraldine Markel
Layout and updated design: Wendy S. Williams
Printed in the United States of America
ISBN 978-0-61541127-9

2008 Edition
College Admissions—from Chaos to Control: A Guide for Students and Families for Solving the College Admissions Puzzle ©2008 by John Boshoven, Debbie Merion & Geraldine Markel
Front & Back Cover Design: Steve Haskin and Elizabeth Sikkenga, Industrial Strength Learning
www.industrialstrengthlearning.com
Document formating: Susie Berneis
Copy Editor: Lisa Nichols

How to Order Additional Copies of this Book (Quantity discounts are available.)
Order paperback from www.managingyourmind.com or Amazon.com
Order PDF from www.managingyourmind.com
Order digital book from www.apple.com/iBooks or Amazon.com for Kindle version.

Contact information for questions, comments, and speaking requests:
www.CollegeAdmissionsAdvisors.com
John Boshoven: boshoven@aaps.k12.mi.us
Debbie Merion: www.EssayCoaching.com   debbie@EssayCoaching.com
Geri Markel: www.managingyourmind.com   www.StudyTipAday   geri@managingyourmind.com

About the Authors

 John B. Boshoven, MA, MSW, LPC, counsels high school students daily in considering possible colleges and finding the right fit. He is a Director of the National Association for College Admission Counseling (NACAC) and Past President of the Michigan Association for College Admission Counseling (MACAC). He is the Counselor for Continuing Education at Community High School/Ann Arbor Public Schools and Founding Director of College Counseling at the Frankel Jewish Academy of Metropolitan Detroit and has a private college counseling practice. His honest and insightful approach endears him to the multitudes of students and parents whom he has helped reduce stress and taught how to control the chaos in college admissions. His email address is boshoven@aaps.k12. mi.us

 Debbie Eisenberg Merion, MFA, MSW, founded Essay Coaching to show students how to write a compelling and successful college essay. Her techniques combine her experience in counseling, teaching college English, and 30 years of professional writing as an award-winning journalist and essayist. Her stories, including interviews with college admissions officers, have been published in the *Ann Arbor Observer, Ann Arbor Business Review, Hour Detroit,* and *Huron River Review.* Whether working one-on-one with students or speaking at in-service teacher training sessions, Debbie delivers clear, commonsense, and compassionate advice. Her email address is debbie@essaycoaching.com and her website is www.essaycoaching.com

Geraldine Markel, PhD, is an educational psychologist who helps students to improve learning and performance. She serves as an academic coach to high school, college, and professional level students. Using research-based strategies and techniques, she helps students of all ages to study better, learn faster, retain more, and show what they know on classroom and high-stakes tests.

Dr. Markel served as faculty at the School of Education, University of Michigan. She is a former history teacher, reading consultant, and special education consultant. Currently principal of Managing Your Mind, she coaches adolescents and adults with AD/HD and/or learning disabilities and presents seminars to improve attention, memory, organization, and other critical thinking skills. She co-authored books such as *Peterson's Parent's Guide to the SAT and ACT* and *Helping Adolescents with ADHD and Learning Disabilities: Practical Tips, Techniques, and Strategies for School Success.* Her email address is geri@managingyourmind.com and her website is www.managingyourmind.com.

You can follow Geri on Twitter http://twitter.com/StudyTipADay or download the Study Tip A Day app at StudyTipADay.com.

Table of Contents

Preface

What do a school counselor, writing coach and academic coach have in common, and why did we write this guide? Here is our story: We all love teens and are in the trenches daily helping them to select and apply to colleges, write effective application essays, and score their best on the ACT or SAT. In addition to our professional training and experience, we have each shepherded our own children through the college admissions process. We understand the questions, fears, and angst.

As an extension of our annual "College Night" at the Ann Arbor District Library, we wrote this guide to bring harmony into your home and reduce the stress around this exciting time.

From students, we hear comments such as:

- "What college should I apply to? There's a big disconnect between my grades and SAT scores. Can I even get in anywhere?"
- "I can't think of anything to write for my application essay."
- "I suck on those timed tests!"
- "I feel so overwhelmed with the pressure—where do I begin?"

From parents, we hear comments such as:

- "I keep telling my son to start writing those applications, but he keeps procrastinating."
- "My daughter's writing is so disorganized. She can't write a short answer on a test, so how can she write an interesting essay for her application?"
- "Thank goodness I didn't have to take the new SATs. I'm not a good test taker, and neither are any of my children. What can they do?"
- "When do we start the application process?"
- "How much should I be involved in this process?"

Based on our success with students and/or their parents, we designed a guide to take the uncertainty and guesswork out of college admissions preparation and decision-making. The four-step process includes:

- Gaining awareness
- Planning and scheduling activities
- Moving from talk to action: completing applications, writing application essays, and studying for tests such as the ACT or SAT
- Taking action with competence and confidence

Here's how our college prep experiences influenced our careers and subsequent commitment to helping students fit together the pieces of the college admissions puzzle.

John Boshoven:

I probably went to the wrong college. I know it now and I knew it then. My dad wouldn't hear my plea to attend a smaller, more social and intimate place. I can say this for my 4-year crawl—I got through it. Author and educator Loren Pope has taught me 25 years later that college shouldn't be something you get through. Rather, it should change your life. Becoming a college counselor may have become my natural reaction to my personal story. I want to help students find colleges that are good fits. In today's competitive college world, my friend Frank reminds me, "College is a match to be made, not a prize to be won."

Debbie Merion:

When I was 17, I had long straight hair parted in the middle, and I hung out with the brainy but fun nerds at Northeast High School in Philadelphia. Although I loved learning and felt that an "A" was the only grade I liked, I had no college counseling to help me understand myself. After I graduated, I wrote computer manuals, published in magazines and taught college English, but inside I yearned to quell the thoughts of "Will it be good enough?" that stopped me developing stories about my own life.

At a writing workshop I learned not to judge the words I scribbled into a stack of journals. I excitedly began to publish my personal essays, and was surprised to hear kudos from editors on the professional stories I submitted. As I reflected on the origin of these fulfilling changes, my sparks of insight, research, and experiences with students fueled the creation of the Essay Coaching writing process. When students are staring at a blank page, I am committed to helping them become more aware of their strengths, find their voices, and craft winning essays as their vehicles to the future.

Geraldine Markel:

Serendipity—chance—led to my college decision and subsequent career. "You ought to go to Michigan. You'll have fun," said a friend I met on the street. I was the first one in my family to go to college, so there was little advice from family except for "Go to college. You need to know how to earn a living." Coming from a non-competitive high school located among factories and under the 59th Street Bridge in New York City, I had better information about Bloomingdale's and the Radio City Music Hall than I did about college. Although I scored well on New York State Regent Examinations, I skipped out of the afternoon SAT Subject Tests because I felt unprepared for them. Luckily, at that time, the University of Michigan did not require a college admission test, and the Ann Arbor campus turned out to be a perfect college fit for me. My unpreparedness for the SAT and fear of non-acceptance, in spite of good grades, however, were experiences not easily forgotten. I think that my commitment to helping students show what they know in school and on high stakes tests stems from my nerve-wracking college prep experience. Now, as the developer of Managing Your Mind Coaching and Seminars and as an academic coach, I reveal to students the system and strategies that yield success. Once students are competent test takers, they become confident students, score higher on tests, and attain greater academic success.

Introduction

In the midst of the college admissions process, the feelings of uncertainty and confusion are similar to the feelings you get when you dump out the pieces of a jigsaw puzzle. With a jigsaw puzzle, you have a picture to refer to before beginning work on the puzzle. When you apply to colleges, however, you often have no vision about what college is like.

In addition, in today's media-frenzied world, going to the BEST college has become a more important factor for many. The rankings have vaulted 100 colleges to "top tier" and "best" categories, with more students thinking they should be admitted to such institutions. Students feel pressure from their families, friends, neighbors and sometimes their high schools.

We designed this guide to give you (and your parents) greater control over the chaos too often triggered during college admissions time. You'll find three sections in this guide to help you.

In Section 1, Finding the College that Fits, you'll gain insight and awareness of what John Boshoven labels "college fit." You, like other students, need to step back and think about what you want and need to get at college, as well as how you can contribute to a college. For example, the size, location, and degree of competitiveness are but a few factors to consider.

In that section you'll find answers to questions such as:
- What are the factors I should consider when looking at colleges?
- When should I begin my college search?
- Who can help me along the way?
- How can I be confident that I'll be admitted to the colleges that fit?

In Section 2, Writing a "Wow" Application Essay, you'll find techniques to find your unique voice and write a winning essay. When you're staring at a blank screen or gripping your pen as you doodle on an empty white sheet of paper, Debbie Merion's section is the place to start.

You'll find answers to questions such as:
- What is the best topic to choose?
- What kind of format do I follow?
- How can I turn my draft into a winning essay?
- What are the college admissions officers really looking for?

In Section 3, Scoring Your Best on Those Nerve-Wracking College Admissions Tests, you'll discover strategies to score high on the ACT or SAT. Tests are an inescapable aspect of school. You need to show what you know by answering multiple choice and essay questions. Although your life is influenced by these "high stakes" tests, many students ignore, procrastinate, or study ineffectively when ACT/SAT time rolls around. Geri Markel outlines short- and long-term activities to move from talk to action and earn your best possible score.

You'll discover answers to questions such as:

- Which tests should I take? • How many times should I take each test?
- How do I sign up for tests?
- How do I deal with test stress?
- What part can my parents play without making me crazy?

This guide helps you move from stress to success. Here are some of the features of the guide:

- Application preparation calendar
- Important tips and techniques missed by many counselors
- Writing exercises for developing a great essay
- Explanations of how to think like an admissions officer
- Common pitfalls and how to avoid them
- A workable plan to prepare for high-stakes tests
- A essential list of references and resources

You, like many students, may wonder where to start. It's not always necessary to read a book from the beginning to the end. You may want to refer back and forth between sections or choose to read only the sections you need as you proceed with the college admissions process.

Following is a handy college preparation checklist to use. If you have friends you like to work with, share it with them and see how they react to the statements about applying to colleges, writing the application essays, and preparing for ACTs or SATs. Work together and learn from and support each other during this process.

College Preparation Checklist

Directions: Read each statement and check any that apply to you.

Those Daunting Applications:

1. I'm unsure about what I should look for in a college.
2. I'll probably wait until the last minute to write my applications.
3. I'm unsure about which colleges to apply to.
4. I'm unsure about how much my grades count in the admission process.
5. I'm unsure about what colleges are looking for.

Those Mystifying Essays:

6. I don't know why colleges want to read an essay.
7. I don't know how to describe my strengths so I don't sound like I'm bragging.
8. I don't know what my "writing voice" is when writing essays.
9. I have a draft, but I don't know how to improve it.
10. I'm not sure about the best length for my essay.

Those Nerve Wracking Tests:

11. I forget what I studied when I take a test.
12. I wait until the last minute to study.
13. I blank out or freeze during tests.
14. I feel rushed when taking tests.
15. I forget to take practice tests.

After completing the checklist:

- Review the list and identify the topic about which you have the most checks.
- Read that section first.
- Talk to your friends, counselor, or family about additional questions or concerns you have after reading other sections.

Use this guide on your own, with a counselor, advisor, coach, or tutor, and with a parent or mentor. Using even a few strategies can help you avoid feeling overwhelmed, rushed, or chaotic—and exert more control over the college preparation process. Hang in and hang on and you'll have more time to hang out.

Best wishes for a productive and enjoyable college prep time!

SECTION I:
Finding the College that Fits

John B. Boshoven, MA, MSW, LPC

How are Students Puzzled by the College Admissions Process?

College applicants are facing an increasing difficult path—namely, rising costs, increased selectivity, and the tyranny of the college rankings. In my day, going to college was the prize. In today's media-frenzied world, going to the BEST college has become a more important factor to many. The rankings have vaulted 100 colleges to "top tier" and "best" categories, leading students to think they should be admitted to such institutions. Students are feeling pressure from their families, friends and neighbors. My students react in several typical ways.

Delay, Delay, Delay—"Put it Off, Buddy!"

Boys are masters of this technique. To be sure, boys typically don't talk about their worries—not to their friends, and certainly not to their parents. "Sure, Mom, I'll get to that soon, but right now I have to go to swimming practice." The chaos and scale of the college search and application process worries high school students, and rather than work it out, it seems easier to put it off. This pushes a really big process into a shorter time frame and causes big decisions to be made quickly, often around the lunch table in senior year. "Where are WE going to college next year?" is often overheard amidst the chewing of cafeteria pizza. Looking for college should not be a group effort. "But, dude, there are 3500 colleges out there, and where do I begin?" The brochures and huge numbers of pieces of mail don't help. Colleges all look alike in these glossy pages—smiling, white-teethed coeds, hunky logo-wearing jocks, beaming sunshine-washed campus greens complete with falling leaves on Dr. McDreamy, the inspirational professor. One Carthage College student confessed to me that it was the brochure that lured him to the campus, where he matriculated. Another Bates College coed confirmed that she was able to keep the sweatshirt after the promotional photo shoot. Be aware that colleges are marketing themselves to you. Shortly after you take your first national standardized test, you will become a target tremendously sought-after, via your mail, email, Facebook, and Twitter.

What Happens if You Put it Off? Worry and Fret

Girls are typically better at acting out their worries and fears than boys. One can overhear their anxiety at the mall or at late-night sleepovers. Unfortunately, hysteria also doesn't always help produce action, but rather keeps the tires of worry and fret spinning. With increasing numbers of women attending college, it could seem that their worry and fret may be helping to motivate better academic performance over their video-gaming male counterparts. Girls outnumber boys at college this year by a 57% to 43% rate, although boys outnumber girls in the U.S. population 51% to 49%. Worry and fret alone, however, will not get a college list or research started.

When is the Best Time to Start the College Search Process?

Some third graders are reading college prep books, but I recommend concentrating on schoolwork through middle school and early high school, and focusing on college during the last two years. Academic success and rigor should begin in freshman year. Sophomore year is a great time to begin thinking about the classes you like and planning for the big picture. The junior year is the "year of the test," so it makes great sense to use that year as the beginning of college planning. Read on, and we'll suggest a process of looking for the college that fits.

How early is too early? A worried student looked up from a computer in our counseling office early in his freshman year, and wondered out loud, "What will they think of ceramics?" I asked who THEY were. "Colleges," he answered. Poor guy. I responded the best I could. Colleges will like you to be well rounded and interesting, and if you are interested in ceramics, they will be, too. I think he was unsatisfied with my answer—he took an extra English class instead. To that lad's credit, however, it's ok to be thinking and talking about college before junior year arrives.

Why are Parents Puzzled?

The admissions chaos has hit Main Street for the past several years, causing parents to worry, hover, dive-bomb and nag. College folks have nicknamed these parents as "helicopter parents," or "fighter jet folks," who swoop down at a moment's notice to rescue Jimmy from the "B" grade, the coach who won't play him enough, or the college admissions officer who didn't admit him. In our day, our parents were instrumental in helping us find and land at a college. Most of us didn't have a long or researched list, but rather a couple of nearby, logical options. Today, parents see the rankings and hear the murmurs at the party or in the stands and are realizing that the college admissions landscape has changed significantly since they applied to college. Bookstores are filled with test-preparation and college admissions materials, the media is keeping us posted regularly, and parents and students alike wonder where to turn for advice and counsel.

Why are Counselors Puzzled?

High school counselors' caseloads have risen dramatically as states grapple with the cost of education. California once sported the highest student-to-counselor ratio, around 900–1 (currently 471–1), but recently other states have seen staggering increases. Michigan's current ratio is 351–1, Arizona's 426–1. The American School Counselor Association recommends a 250–1 ratio, instead of today's national average of 479–1. High school counseling offices deal with the many stresses of today's high school students—divorce, depression, drug/alcohol abuse, class scheduling, dropouts, suicide, and of course post high school and college counseling. However, there is relatively little training for high counselors about college counseling Few graduate schools offer a course in college counseling as part of the required training. Until graduate schools see the high school-to-college transition as a worthy subject and public high school administrators see college counseling as a strategic priority, public school counselors will continue to struggle to keep up with the ever-changing college admission and financial aid landscape.

Why College?

Yesterday's entry-level jobs after high school (clerk, cashier, sales clerk, teller, and factory worker) either are outsourced today to cheaper labor markets or require a college degree. In the last several years, two- and four-year colleges and universities have seen a record number of applications and enrollments, thanks to an influx of baby boomers' children and lack of employment options for those with only a high school diploma. Yesterday's high school diploma is today's college degree. These days, it should not be IF I go on for further training and education, but rather what I want to learn and where I want to learn beyond high school. As a high school counselor, I urge every high school graduate to seek training and education at the next level. Students with college degrees can expect to earn upwards of a million dollars more than their non-college-educated friends in their lifetimes. Without a college diploma, students will experience more difficulty in finding jobs that pay health and medical benefits or that offer any kind of advancement. Without college, students will simply need to learn one simple phrase: "Do you want fries with that?"

What are Colleges & Universities Looking for in their Future Students?

Colleges are looking for strong academic achievement with a challenging curriculum, involvement in school and community, growth and initiative with special interests and talents, and competitive scores on standardized tests.

Strong Academic Preparation & Achievement (Depth)

College admission officers look first of all at the depth of your knowledge, in terms of good grades and a strong, deep curriculum. For example, if you like Spanish, take four years of a languages when only two or three might be required. The curriculum depth and Grade Point Average (GPA) are gleaned from the high school transcript, which is your academic record throughout high school. Students should seek as much academic study as possible, including during the senior year. Students are also using the summer months to do interesting things as well as taking classes. Students should not be "dumbing down" in the senior year: they don't YET deserve an academic break! For the most selective colleges, take four years of math, science, social studies, English and world language to make sure your transcript is as deep as possible. Good grades and depth of subjects are vital to giving you the most options for college admission. Ask your counselor to allow you to review your transcript regularly. Be sure there are no errors or omissions. This is the single most important document the college will evaluate in your application materials because it shows the patterns of your academic performance. It is the demonstration of work ethic and achievement over a four-year period, which is seen as crucial for college completion as well.

Academic and Community Interests (Breadth)

Secondly, pay attention to your breadth of knowledge: take interesting classes with the best teachers. If your teacher doesn't match your learning style and/or preferences, seek a different one. Remember, you only do high school once! The more engaged you are with your teacher, the better you'll do in the class. The more relevant the subject becomes, the better you'll do and the more you will enjoy it at the same time. If science isn't your bag, take an extra English class. Try to go beyond what your high school curriculum offers. Get involved in your community and world. Service, involvement in your faith community, scouting, athletics, political action or theater all can round out your academic record. Colleges seek active and ethical citizens to contribute to the fabric of their campus communities, so don't just read books in your bedroom during high school. Get involved and be as academically interesting as possible! For example, if you like animals, try volunteering at your local animal shelter.

Academic Rigor (Stretch)

You stretch when you take an AP course, and meet the increased rigor that advanced classes provide. Most college count the number of AP and honor classes you have taken in relationship to the amount offered in your school. However, don't be overload yourself with too many of these courses leaving no time for other activities.

Your high school prepares a document that describes the academic features of your school on its high school Profile, which your high school sends along with your transcript to the colleges where you are applying. The Profile explains what and how many advanced classes (AP, IB, Honors, ACC, etc.) your school offers, as well as the grading system your high school employs. The more rigorous the classes you succeed in, the more admissions options you will have. Ask your counselor to allow you to review your school's Profile so you will know how your application may be viewed. One student's public school's Profile was filled with spelling and typographical errors. He was subsequently instrumental in helping his school improve its Profile before it accompanied his application documents to college. Some high schools do not actively work with the colleges to explain the uniqueness of their schools or classes. If this is the case with your school, you might need to help the college admission officer where you're applying to better understand your community and school.

Quality Instruction (Context)

The context, i.e. the academic environment of your high school, is considered in your application and is important to the college admission officer. College applications ask your counselor to report your school's average test scores and college-bound rates. Admissions offices keep track of the college success of past matriculates from your high school. The better the high school preparation, the more favorable later applicants from your school will be viewed. Find out from your counselor whether students from your school have applied and been admitted to the colleges on your list, and whether college representatives visit your high school or the area. Develop a relationship with the college admission representatives—they can be helpful to you. They know their schools and can answer particular questions you have and connect you with valuable and helpful campus resources. The representative is also often the first reader of your application at his/her college. If s/he knows you and your school, this can definitely help you gain admission to the college that fits you best.

Talent

Are you applying to music, theater or art school? Perhaps you're interested in engineering, architecture, or nursing. Are you an athlete? These college applications may require auditions, portfolios, or particular high school training. Each college's program will specify its particular requirements, which can rival the transcript in importance in landing an admission offer. Getting started early is the best insurance that you will have ample time to produce quality pieces for your application. Scheduling early auditions is advised, as spaces can fill up before you've ever been heard or seen. Art portfolio seminars offered in the junior year or summers can be particularly helpful to art students. Engineering and architecture schools often require more math, science and drawing as preparation, whereas nursing schools have become more interested in healthcare experiences before college application, such as volunteering, caring for an ill relative or taking health-related coursework. For college-bound athletes, you will want to be working with the college coach alongside of the admissions office throughout the application and decision process.

What Should Students Look for in a College?

Twelfth grade students are flooding into counselors' offices in record numbers and madly looking for the right college to attend. The stress and anxiety can be palpable! But, let's be sensible—it's not marriage we're proposing here! College is not a lifetime commitment, but rather a two- to six-year one. There isn't necessarily the perfect college for you. A school doesn't have to meet every minute specification, but it should give a student what he/she is looking for. College is like a coat. Finding the right college should meet the same specifications as shopping for a new coat. Please consider that the important steps in researching take time. Students and families should be fully engaged in the process no later than the junior year—the earlier, the better. Don't believe me? Simply look at the stressed faces of most high school seniors as they race to find and apply to colleges at the last minute. That's where too many students settle for baggy sweatshirts rather than a well-fitted coat.

Proper research can prevent an expensive mistake. Like shopping for a coat, buying one from a mail-order catalog can be risky, especially if the buyer isn't exactly sure of the sleeve length, collar size, etc. Sears has figured this out, and now features mail-order clothes, in the store, from catalog king Lands End. My wife, with her unusual shoe size, can expect mail order to take 2–3 roundtrips before the fit is right. Who of us hasn't noticed that clothes labeled the same size, even on the same rack, aren't always identical? The same goes with the college search. One size does not fit all. How can you know if it fits? Try it on! Visit the college with your parents and/or friends; talk to kids, professors, admission folks. Visit classes and team practices. Take the tour and talk to students around the campus.

Students with learning disabilities or who are physically challenged need to ask particular questions about services, facilities and/or special programs. Resources like the K & W Guide to Schools for Learning Disabled and ADD Students can help identify particular schools with more structured and organized programs to assist students. Many students seek study abroad options or alternative spring break and community service opportunities at college.

What are the Factors Crucial to Finding a Good Coat or College?

The same criteria that you use to find a good coat help you decide on a good college for you. You'll look at fit, feel, flair, and cost and function.

How Does the College Fit?

"Know thyself," taught the ancient philosopher Plato. When applied in today's world, this means understand what you want and need from your college. Loren Pope (2007) writes, "Picking a college is a crucial decision because the experience profoundly affects the quality of one's future life. It can be the most exciting four years of your life. On the other hand, you can plod through largely untouched and unaffected, or drop out, or fail. Most teenagers give more thought to learning to drive or water ski than to picking a college." Commit yourself to spending time on this very important project.

Since most teens simply go to the public school in their zip code, they are lulled into thinking that education is simply a mass-choice event. "No big deal—one college is like another," they surmise. I have worked in two small high schools (one public and one private), and have gained a keen appreciation for what a smaller setting can do for the right student. One student recently told me, "I like my school because my teachers all know me well, can encourage me, and can help me when I have problems. I also like being in a community of learners; there's a lot of trust here." My daughter was excited by the adventure; she sought out colleges to which few students from her high school had ever applied, and found a small liberal arts college that was perfect. "Everyone in class knows my name, and we talk about class all over campus, including at dinner. Unfortunately my high school counselor didn't know the college at all so I had to do most of the work myself." My son sought out a larger environment in which he could be more invisible and anonymous, and happily graduated not knowing any of his teachers well. Another student from a huge public high school had quite a less positive view of his experience: "My high school is like a factory; my counselor has no idea who I am."

If a college/university seems too big, check out whether it offers any small residential learning communities. These options are becoming more popular and can be designated as theme houses, honors programs, language houses or community service programs. Studies show that students do better academically when they engage with other students in smaller settings. That can also happen in a club, music group, band or intramural sporting activity.

Another important factor that distinguishes smaller from larger colleges is the graduation rate. Small colleges post 4-year graduation rates which are often much higher than big colleges' 6-year rates, so beware. Sticker prices are different, but with added years of study come additional expenses and loss of potential earnings. Small colleges support ALL students graduating in four years, while big colleges sometimes say, "What's the rush?"

In addition to size, there are other factors of fit to consider. For example:

- What kind of social atmosphere am I seeking?
- I am looking for a more liberal than conservative place.
- I hope to find a fraternity to join.
- I want to be in the middle of a big city.
- I want to be active in a faith community.
- I want to be no more than two hours drive from home.
- I want to yodel and climb mountains.

Students should begin their searches by taking stock of themselves and their reasons for going to college. Since they spend only about 20% of their time on campus in class, for the sake of the 80% spent elsewhere, the college should be a good social fit. Participating in the band, playing sports, rock climbing, or squirrel watching—special social outlets will better ensure a happy and connected college life. My son reminded me that he had a couple of "free" mornings each week. I urged him to consider these as "otherwise engaged in all things academic" days.

In your search for the right college, it shouldn't be the perfect college you're seeking, since there is no such thing, but rather a good fit. Students who find this fit are happier. Happier students do better in college. Happier students graduate. That's the point!

How Does the College Feel?

"The first time I visited Oberlin, it just felt right!" I have heard similar stories from students on over 200 college campuses. What feels right to one student may feel wrong to another. You may think I look good in my new coat, but only I know how it feels. It might feel tight or scratchy. "Trying on" colleges requires college visits. You can't feel the atmosphere from a brochure or another person's experience. Talking to college representatives, students and faculty will make the difference in how a place feels. One senior recently told me about a college I suggested, "It's a fine college that has the academic program I want, but when I visited it just didn't feel right." My son remarked in returning from what had been his #1 college for a second visit, "I liked it better when the students weren't there." Another, returning from a weekend visit, scowled, "I didn't see enough students like me." I smiled. Aren't you glad you found this out now rather than later?

How does the College Look on You? (Fashion/Flair)

"That college really seems to suit you," I recently told my returning graduate, a freshman at Lawrence University. Smiling, he said, "Yes, I think we're a good pair." College needs to look good on our students—namely, do good things for them. Students should love the idea of going to a college, even if their best friends, counselors or parents have never heard of it. Brian was thrilled to attend Grinnell College, even though his best friend had thought he meant Cornell!

Counselors should propose a range of fitting options, from the "stretch" to the more "sure thing." We used to call more sure choices "safety schools"—schools you're confident you can get into. Wesleyan Dean Barbara Jan Wilson warns, "We don't call them safeties anymore, because NOBODY wants to go to their safety school." Rather, counselors can help students find colleges that admit students with the same general range of grades, scores and backgrounds. A 12th grader called me and asked about his admission chances at some Ivies and other very selective eastern schools. I advised him to widen his list of eight because I didn't think he was a shoe-in any of them. He was rejected from 8 of his 9 schools, and luckily for him, I had suggested the 9th, Connecticut College. "Who advised you on your list of those eight?" I asked. "No one," he scowled.

The fashion and flare have to match you, the student—not your girlfriend, parents or counselor. Ultimately, students should be proud about where they go to college. For many, this could be the community college or state university, which might be a good deal cheaper, compared to a four-year private college/university. If you've done your homework and given yourself plenty of time, you should be in your first choice school in October in your freshman year in college.

How Much Does it Cost?

Students sometimes need to be reminded that college is a costly enterprise. Parents have gotten this picture clearly. After my own admission to college in the spring of my senior year in high school, I finally had the "money talk" with my father. At that moment he "sprung" the fact that he couldn't/wouldn't afford the school that was my clear first choice, and that if I wanted him to pay for college, it was the state school or nothing. I "trudged" to the school that didn't fit me, and struggled through it. Survive I did, but I could have had a very different talk with my dad. Three facts that I know now, but didn't know then:

- Private colleges give more money in merit aid than public universities.

- I could help support myself at college by working summers and at college where work-study jobs are pretty easy to land.

- I could take on a loan or three. My dad certainly knew about that option and could have easily been helpful had I sought that help because he was a commercial loan officer in our city's largest bank.

With respect to college, often you get what you pay for. The state university's mission to educate the "masses" more cheaply may not be the best fit for every student. My son didn't mind his huge classes, but my daughter would have fled a chemistry class with 1200 students. I had GSIAs (graduate student instructors) who didn't speak the mother tongue, and I struggled to understand the material. My son sought an atmosphere that fostered anonymity, and didn't want to know the students sitting around him or the faculty up front. My friend recounted the first-day speech by his professor. "Take a look at the person on either side of you—one of you will be gone next year and the other will be gone the following year." This competition thrilled him, and he vowed to be the survivor. He lasted two years. Consider carefully what kind of atmosphere you can expect to thrive in. Also, ask prospective colleges about their four-year graduation rates. Smaller liberal arts colleges commit to graduating the vast majority in four years, whereas state universities sometimes don't sport an enviable six-year graduation rate. Adding years to college study is a costly prospect.

What are Some Other Practical/Personal Considerations?

Your college should work, that is, it should function for you, just like a coat must be warm and waterproof if it's to be a good purchase. If you're a history buff, attending Kettering University, Georgia Tech or Cal Arts won't work because they don't offer much history. Students should carefully research whether the programs they want are available at the colleges on their list, and choose accordingly. Unsure about what you want? Pick colleges or universities that will allow you to explore, wander and otherwise "shop." Some colleges, like the University of Chicago, have a strong core curriculum, requiring students to take several classes in 4–5 subject areas, thus encouraging students to explore more deeply. Other colleges have no core requirements. At Brown, you can graduate after passing 32 history classes if you like! First and foremost, find a college that provides the range of subjects you might require. A student recently told me she had to transfer because her college didn't offer the major she wanted. Transferring is expensive, inconvenient and counterproductive. Do your homework first!

How Can Students Research the "Fit?"

Here are ten steps to discover the "fit" of a college. Among other things, you can read brochures, talk to family and friends, talk to college reps, contact each college on your list, and visit the college.

First: Read

Read what the colleges say about themselves. A college's own brochures, website and course catalog can give you a picture of what it is most proud of or known for. Look for information such as freshmen retention rate, and transfer rate, or driving rules for students. These facts can give you a sense of how residential the college is, or whether it is a suitcase college on the weekends. Explore the depth of programs you are interested in. For example, if a college has only one "strings" teacher, you can surmise that music is not its strong suit! Read the student newspaper to find out about what students describe as their current issues and concerns. One eastern college vice president told our assembled group of counselors that lack of parking was the primary concern of students. The headline in the student newspaper disagreed. It screamed of high crime statistics and poor neighborhood relations.

Use a guidebook to read what other people say about the college. My favorite, Edward Fiske's The Fiske Guide to Colleges, reminds us that this country has an enormously rich and varied network of colleges and universities. "There are dozens of institutions out there that can meet the need of any particular student. Too many students approach the college selection process wearing blinders, limiting their sights to local institutions, the pat schools of their parents or guidance counselors, or to ones they may know by possibly outdated reputations."

Second: Get Good Help with the College Admissions Process

If you're the oldest child in your family to attend college, remember your parents haven't done a college search in a while. When they did it, the landscape was very different. Some parents never went to college. Seeking extra help may help turn chaos into control. Who can help?

Parents and Relatives

If an older brother or sister went off to college, then your parents may have recent and relevant experiences to share about how they helped. The process and ultimate college choice may be different for each child, but family members may be able to offer sound advice about timing, visiting, essays, etc. Perhaps an uncle or aunt has recently assisted a cousin. They, too, can be helpful. Your friends' parents may also have relevant experience and interest.

School Counselor

Chances are, if he/she is experienced, your counselor can be a regular source of helpful and reasonable information. A good counselor can help explain dates and deadlines, the application process, and the school's processes for completing the application, as well as offering tips on majors, essays, colleges and scholarships. Be aware that most guidance counselors have never had a course in college counseling, so the amount of help provided may be uneven among counselors. Is there a more experienced college counselor at your school you can work with? Is there a career or college counselor employed in your school or district who has more recent and relevant experience? Seek out the best help available.

An Independent Counselor/Consultant

Advice from seasoned professionals is available in virtually every community in America. These independent counselors are often guidance counselors who have amassed a great deal of college counseling experience. They can be useful in developing a personal family timeline, college lists, helping you deal with scholarships and financial aid. They can also assist you to work best with your school guidance counselor. Ask around. Word of mouth is often the best way to find a counselor who can help.

Third: Talk to Your People

Looking for college is similar to looking for a dentist. Word of mouth (pun intended)—testimonials from people who know and love you and know colleges—can reinforce your confidence in a college that looks like a good fit. Conversely, a trusted source can give advice to shorten your list. Often these important contacts can suggest some additional colleges to consider. Pick the brains of your parents, family, friends' parents, counselors and teachers. You can't rely on your friends here—they're as lost as you are! Some questions to consider include:

1) Why do you think Fabulous U is right for you?

2) What kinds of students do best at Fab U?

3) What do/did you like best about going there?

4) What would you change about the place?

5) What other schools might you suggest I add to my list?

While walking on a beach adjacent to his college, I asked my former student Chris how he heard about New College of Florida. He smiled. "You told me about it, John." Sure enough, when I got home and reviewed my notes from his junior conference, it was third from the bottom! Personal recommendations can make for positive results.

Fourth: Talk to the Representatives of the Colleges Themselves

Colleges and university representatives visit selected high schools and conduct evening meetings at area schools, hotels and living rooms. Many colleges assign admissions staff regionally who actually get to know the context of your application (your city, school and counselor). These regional representatives actually read your application, should you apply. A representative from Barnard College told me, of one student, "If she's anything on paper like she is in person, I want her on my campus." The college admitted her and she went on to graduate! Getting to know these important college representatives can help you get to know the college better, and can help the college to get to know you, the applicant, better. Colleges are looking for students who fit them; at the same time you're seeking a good fit for you in a college.

Check out area college fairs. Sure, they are crowded and loud, but they provide yet another opportunity to spend time with your representative. One Wittenberg University student told me that the conversation she had with the young man at the Bloomfield Hills college fair I recommended was instrumental in her subsequent application and matriculation with a generous scholarship.

Meet with your regional representative when you visit a college, if only for a friendly cup of coffee. Many colleges track contacts they have with prospective students and are careful to consider who will be offered the space for the fall. Those students who have done a more conscientious job in researching their prospective college may have a better chance of having the seat offered to them.

Fifth: Contact each College/University on Your List

Email your prospective colleges' representatives to learn more about their programs and opportunities. Request materials and become identified as a prospective student ("prospie"). Getting on school' lists of "prospies" will allow representatives to notify you when they are visiting your school or area. Ask representatives to link you with current students at their institutions who may share your interests. My daughter heard from tennis-playing, science major flute players! Ask representatives to link you with college faculty who can talk about your academic interests and opportunities. The students and faculty should become your college experts! One Carnegie Mellon University professor told me, "I love to talk with students about their opportunities here and at other great schools—send 'em my way." A University of Michigan professor reinforced this sentiment: "I love what I do and am happy to talk to anyone who is interested, whether or not they end up coming to Michigan."

Sixth: Visit the College(s)

Yes, kiss the bricks! For perhaps the first time, you are actually picking your classmates and professors, as well as the city and campus environments. Look for clubs and organizations to be involved with; visit classes in session; talk to faculty and admissions officers. Check out the campus center and recreational facilities. After many hours, you'll have a better "feel" of the place. Ask students and faculty:

- What do you like about this place?
- What was the biggest surprise when you first arrived?
- What other schools did you consider?
- Why did you choose this school?
- What's one thing you would change?
- What's a current campus interest or concern?
- Why should I come here?

Seventh: Narrow Your Choices

Once your research is complete, you should have a good list of fewer than ten colleges to which to consider applying. Seek help from your school and/or independent counselor to determine which choices are good fits (schools you think you have a great shot at). Since you will want to apply to more schools that will admit you than those that will reject you. It's fine to apply to a couple of "stretch" schools (schools you are not sure will admit you), but you don't deserve to be rejected from more colleges than you're accepted by. The college application process should be an affirming and happy culmination of a successful high school career, not an ego-bruising experience.

Eighth: Apply

Typically, students apply to between four to eight colleges. Don't let your number creep up too high, as it costs $50–$70 apiece to apply to colleges these days. Consider a 2–1 ratio of "fit" to "stretch" schools. Watch deadlines, apply early for rolling-admission colleges, and consider the early application programs (see below) if a college surfaces as your clear first choice. Make copies of everything. Be sure the college has received all of your complete application materials even when applying on-line. Several of my students had their applications delayed because a letter of recommendation or supplement wasn't received or was lost at the college or the student failed to press the submit command.

A note about waiting:
Waiting is something we don't do well. Use your waiting time to search for scholarships while still concentrating on your important senior year schoolwork. Remember, your grades still count in senior year.

Admissions offers arrive in all shapes and sizes—large, clever, overt, subtle. One student simply received a luggage tag emblazoned with the Northwestern University logo. Another got an invitation to the admitted students' weekend at Kenyon, while another opened a letter to find confetti streaming down. If you've done your homework right, you'll have good news coming, but there's still work to do.

Ninth: Compare the Offers

One Stanford University freshman told me, "I didn't really want to look too seriously at colleges until I knew they wanted me. I didn't want to fall in love and get left at the altar (mailbox, in this case). It was after the acceptances came where I really put my heart and soul into my college visits. Turns out, one of my first early choices I ended up not liking. I was able to compare the offers (financial, program, campus, location) and found that some of my priorities had changed the closer I got to the final decision."

I have traveled to hundreds of college campuses. When I speak to students, I always ask why they ultimately chose the colleges they were attending. I can count on hearing two common reasons, among a host of others. First, students say:

My financial package made this college more affordable

At first, I was surprised to hear students based their decision on price. I expected this to be their parents' sentiments, but the students seem to translate a good financial package into meaning, for instance, "The College of Wooster wanted me more than other colleges did." The stress of the application process takes a lot out of students who are questioning their worth along the way. It doesn't help that the "uber"-selective colleges have turned the application process into a supplication process. In the end, having an admissions offer is an ego-strengthener. A better financial offer boosts this self-esteem ever more, and I'm sure the parents are more than happy to reinforce this expression of love and acceptance. I also hear students say:

It just "felt right"

Throughout the "trying-on" period, there is a "comfort" need—a need to find a college that "feels" good. This is almost a spiritual feeling of welfare, rather than a tangible, fact-driven experience. When I visited Bates, Bowdoin and Colby, three small liberal arts colleges in Maine whose geography and student characteristics are relatively similar, I still found students talking about how the "feel" of one in particular was better suited to them. Was it the sunny day of the visit, the hunky tour guide, the cafeteria meal? It probably all plays a hand in a student's sense of the feel of the joint.

I remember my son's sour "feeling" after touring some colleges in Rochester, NY, one spring day. "Too much snow," he groused. Rochester had just happened to get 8 inches that day. Funny, when looking at some Ohio colleges in the days that followed, the weather had warmed and the sun had returned, and he had a better "feeling" about a couple of those. Warning: don't let a bad tour guide or sloppy day make your decision. You might want to come back another time and try the place on again. I asked Whitman College's Dean of Admissions to give me a second tour guide after the first one severely disappointed me. I knew the college was a lot better than the impression given by my less-than-stellar student guide.

Tenth: Continue Your Research to Make a Commitment

Revisit the college. Staying in the dorm and eating in the cafeteria is important on your return (or first and last) visit. One of my students returned after her decision weekend, and announced that she hated it. I told her I was glad she had spent the weekend. It wasn't an hour later that the Director of Admissions called and echoed the sentiment that the student and his college were not a good match. The student and the institution simply were not compatible.

Hopefully , at this point, you are heading down the home stretch. Still can't decide? That probably means you have too many good options! Counselors and parents can be helpful at this juncture by suggesting pro/con scales, weighted or un-weighted. If you imagine making a decision and finding after a year that it was the wrong one, which college left on the list would be the hardest to transfer to? That might be the school to start with. The parents of one student glared at me when I offered that suggestion, for it meant I had just given their daughter permission to try out the University of Texas at Austin, rather than the safer, closer Indiana University. Another senior was so undecided, I suggest she go home and "announce" one of the two colleges as the winner, and see how she felt in the morning, having made this public declaration. She returned in the morning much relieved. "I can't wait to go to Smith," she smiled. Later that fall, she thanked me profusely for helping her decide. All I did was ask her to declare, and that fueled her decision.

NOW—It is time to make the commitment and say, "I do!"

Remember, it's not marriage, but making that final decision to accept can be such an exciting event—one laced with expectation, anxiety and relief. Go out for ice cream—wear the college sweatshirt to school. Celebrate!

What are Options for Admission?

Once you've made your college choice, you have options. Some colleges offer programs of "early decision," "early action," or "early response." You'll want to know the details surrounding each of these special categories of admission. There are options too, in case you have a late start. Consider and discuss with your family the various options.

Early Decision

Early Decision (ED) is a binding contract among student, family and college. It is like a proposal of marriage initiated by the student's application. If accepted, the student agrees to attend this "first choice" college and withdraw all other college applications. These applications are typically made in early November of the senior year, and the colleges will decide by around December 20. Once the college says yes, and the family has agrees to the terms, both financial and exclusionary, the student is required to accept the offer. Some students are using this as a strategy, because they feel their chances for acceptance is greater if they promise to lock-in early. Early Decision is designed for students who have a clear and unequivocal first choice college. This December decision deadline does not allow the student or family to compare financial aid offers from any other schools, since all other applications have been withdrawn.

Early Action

Early Action (EA), also known as Early Response, is a non-binding program announcing to colleges that the applicant favors this particular school, but will not need to decide until the regular admission decision date of May 1st. The college will render an admissions decision around December 20, and the student has until May to decide, allowing him the opportunity to compare financial offers down the road and to further decide about priorities. This win-win program, unfortunately, is offered by a relatively small number of colleges. There's no clear advantage to the college here, since it can't "lock up" the space.

Wait-list or Deferred Decisions

Students are applying to more and more schools these days. Electronic applications and use of universal applications, such as the Common Application (www.commonapp.org), allow students to apply to a larger number of schools more easily (I did not say more cheaply). With this ease of applying, colleges are faced with larger numbers of applicants who are themselves facing more decisions. Admission offices are never certain who will accept their offers, so they use a complex mathematical formula, based on past admission yield trends and current market conditions. In an effort to better manage this yield, some colleges are tightly managing this admission stream and using wait lists to keep potential matriculates "in the pool" while waiting for others to decide. A counselor can be particularly helpful in guiding you through this wait list purgatory, should you find yourself there. If any of your favorite schools put you on a waiting list and you want to keep them as options:

- Notify them via email, web and phone that you are willing to be considered later.

- Keep them posted about your continued interest along the way.

- Inform them of recent happenings, awards, grades, recognitions and news since your initial application.

Ultimately, they may have a space or two to offer, and they want to offer such a spot to the student who's most likely to take it. Maintaining communication and reaffirming your interest reassures a school of your intention. Conversely, if you have decided that your right school is a different one, let others know to cut you loose so they can offer that seat to another student.

Late/Early Starts

Regardless of when the student is admitted, the student has some options of when to start. From the college's perspective, allowing students to begin college in the summer before or the semester after ensures that every bed is taken in the college residence hall. Dartmouth was probably the first college to popularize this program, calling it the D Plan. This plan allows students to creatively plan and study abroad, and it ensures the sophomore class will all be on campus in the summer. Management and usage of expensive residence hall property is a driving force for many of these colleges' decisions. Colleges are forced to ensure the highest occupancy rates. My son's friend was offered an early June start at Michigan. He accepted and never looked back. He was already an oriented freshman by the time the rest of the class arrived in August. Another student happily accepted a January start at Florida State, allowing him to travel and work for a semester to earn extra pizza and book money.

Who Should Write Letters of Recommendation?

Selective colleges and universities require a counselor recommendation and one or two recommendations from academic teachers.

Counselor letter(s)

Remember to ask your counselor to write a letter for you if required by the college. Often, counselors will ask their students to fill out a questionnaire highlighting their accomplishments and activities. You can help you counselor write a more personal letter if you spend more time together, helping him or her to know you better. There may by other adults who know you well (relatives, bosses, coaches, religious leaders, etc.) who might be willing to send your counselor a paragraph or two about you—information from such sources can help the counselor round out your letter. Please remember to thank him/her for helping with your applications and give them plenty of time to prepare your letter.

Teacher letter(s)

Ask your teacher(s) early. Some teachers appreciate a listing of the classes you've taken with them and any samples of your work that can help them better remember you. Supply a stamped, addressed envelope or the email link for each college where you are applying. Remember to thank these teachers for their help—and remember to follow up with them to be sure the task was accomplished!

Other letters

Perhaps you are active in scouting, athletics, music, drama or your faith community. You may have held down a steady job or been an active volunteer in your community. Perhaps you've won an award or two. Additional letters of recommendation demonstrating a different area of your life away from school can also help admissions officers get to know another part of you—a part they are also interested in, since you will also (hopefully) be involved in extracurricular activities while you are away at college. You are more than simply grades and test scores.

Suppose it Doesn't Fit?

What if you make the wrong decision or run out of money? My A lonely homesick Occidental freshman called in November and asked me to guide her through the transfer process. I told her to call me in June and I would happily assist. In the meantime, I suggested she get involved in at least one club or activity. In March, she called and was having the time of her life. "I love it here," she exclaimed. Get involved and give yourself a year before considering a transfer. If transfer becomes necessary, you already know how to research and try on the next coat!

What are 10 Tips for Finding a College that Fits?

1. Start early by talking to college counselors, reading brochures, and visiting campuses.

2. Understand that colleges look for students with academic and community interests, academic achievement, talent, and special interests.

3. Look for campuses on which you feel comfortable, like trying on a comfortable shirt.

4. Consider the costs and the possibilities of financial aid or scholarships.

5. Talk to others (your people) to find their view of a school and whether they see you on that campus. Your people include family, and friends, students, teachers, counselors, independent counselors or consultants, and representatives of colleges.

6. Contact each college or university on your list and visit as many as possible, learning about any early admission opportunities.

7. Discuss letters of recommendations from your school counselor, teacher, or supervisor of an internship, work experience, or volunteer activity.

8. Apply to 4 – 8 colleges, watching deadlines, editing for spelling and grammatical mistakes, and making copies of everything.

9. Compare offers in terms of comfort, interests, costs, and academic offerings and perhaps, revisiting the college.

   Make the final decision, knowing that you did the best you could and that if you made the wrong decision or run out of money, you have options of transferring.

Conclusion

Selecting the best college for you is like a selecting the right coat. The right college experience can improve your life! Make sure you do your research to find the right place for the next four years—a college that fits, looks good on you, feels good, works and is affordable. Enjoy learning and college life. Remember that the college degree will take you to the next level—graduate school, employment, and/or further training! Happy college shopping.

College Planning Schedule

Junior Year

Begin college selection process. Attend college fairs, financial aid seminars, general information sessions, etc., to learn as much as you can about the college application process. Make sure you are meeting NCAA requirements if you want to play Division I, II or III sports in college.

August/September

- Register for the October Preliminary SAT (PSAT). Meet with your guidance/college counselor or forum leader to review your courses for this year and plan your schedule for senior year.

- Save samples of your best work for your academic portfolio (all year).

- Maintain your co-curricular record (all year).

October

- Junior year PSAT scores may qualify a student for the National Merit Scholarship Competition and the National Achievement or National Hispanic Scholars Programs. Even though these scores will not be used for college admissions, it is still a good idea to take the PSAT. The more times you take standardized tests, the more familiar you will become with the format and the types of questions asked. If you wish to receive free information from colleges, indicate on the PSAT test answer form that you want to participate in the Student Search. A useful report will arrive at your high school in early December for your review.

November

- Junior year grades are extremely important in the college admission process, because they are a measure of how well you do in advanced, upper-level courses. Grades also are used to determine scholarships and grants for which you may be eligible. So put in the extra effort and keep those grades up!

- If you will require financial aid, start researching your options for grants, scholarships and work-study programs. Make an appointment with your counselor, or start by visiting National Association for College Admission Counseling's (NACAC) Web Resources for the College-Bound (www.nacacnet.org) to do research on your own using the Internet.

December

- During December you should receive the results of your PSAT. Read your score report and consult your school counselor to determine how you might improve on future standardized tests. The PSAT is excellent preparation for the SAT Reasoning Test, which you will take in the spring.

January

- Begin to make a preliminary list of colleges you would like to investigate further. Surf the net and use the college resources in the guidance office or library.

- Ask your parents for your Social Security number (required on many college applications). If you were never issued a Social Security number, contact the closest Social Security office as soon as possible to obtain a number.

February

- Meet with your guidance/college counselor to discuss your preliminary list of colleges. Discuss whether your initial list of colleges meets your needs and interests (academic program, size, location, cost, etc.) and whether you are considering colleges where you are likely to be admitted. You should be optimistic and realistic when applying to colleges.

- Register for the March SAT Reasoning Test if you have completed the math courses covered on the SAT Reasoning Test. If not, plan to take the SAT Reasoning Test in May or June. Prepare for the SAT Reasoning Test or ACT by signing up for a prep course, using computer software, or doing the SAT/ACT practice tests available in the counseling office or at bookstores. But don't spend so much time trying to improve standardized test scores that your grades and co-curricular involvement suffer.

March

- Many states have state comprehensive exams like New York's Regent Exams or Michigan's Merit Exam (MME). The MME contains the ACT, ACT Work Keys and various other tests that will judge your academic profile as well as the schools'. The ACT is a college-reportable score, so it will "count" as the real deal, with NO CHARGE to you or your hard-working parent(s).

- Write, telephone, or use the Internet to request admission literature and financial aid information from the colleges on your list. There is no charge and no obligation to obtain general information about admission and financial aid.

April

- Attend a college fair to get more information about colleges on your list. NACAC sponsors college fairs in cities across the country. Visit the National Association for College Admission Counseling (NACAC) National College Fairs Web page (www. nacacnet.org) to check out the schedule for the National College Fairs and the Performing and Visual Arts College Fairs.

- When selecting your senior courses, be sure to continue to challenge yourself academically.

- Register for the May/June SAT Reasoning Test, ACT and/or the May/June SAT Subject Tests. Not all SAT Subject Tests are given on every test date. Check the calendar carefully to determine when the Subject Tests you want are offered.

- Continue to evaluate your list of colleges and universities. Eliminate colleges from the original list that no longer interest you, and add others as appropriate.

- Look into summer jobs or apply for special summer academic or enrichment programs. Colleges love to see students using their knowledge and developing their skills and interests.

May

- Get a jump-start on summer activities—consider enrolling in an academic course at a local college, pursuing a summer school program, applying for an internship, working, or volunteering. If you work, save part of your earnings for college.

- Begin/continue visiting colleges. Phone to set up appointments. Interviews are always a good idea. Many colleges will tell you they are optional, but an interview will show interest, enthusiasm and initiative on your part and provide an excellent opportunity to have your questions answered. Do a practice interview with your counselor, teacher, employer, or a senior who has had college interviews. Set up interviews as early as possible—interview times become booked quickly!

- Take the SAT Reasoning Test or the SAT Subject Tests.

June

- After school ends, get on the road to visit colleges. Seeing the college firsthand, taking a tour and talking to students can be the greatest help in deciding whether or not a school is right for you. Although it is ideal to visit colleges during the academic year, going in the summer will be valuable. Admission offices employ current students to give tours and answer questions from prospective students and their parents.

- Take the SAT Reasoning Test, the SAT Subject Tests and/or the ACT.

July

- Visit colleges, take tours, have interviews, and ask questions. Make college visiting a family event. Involve your parents and siblings in every step of your application process. Choosing the right college is a tough decision; the opinions of those who know you best can provide helpful insight into which college is best for you.

August

- Continue to refine your list of potential colleges and universities.

- Begin preparing for the actual application process: draft application essays, collect writing samples, and assemble portfolios or audition tapes. If you are an athlete and plan on playing in college, contact the coaches at the schools to which you are applying and ask about intercollegiate and intramural sports programs and athletic scholarships.

- Complete the NCAA Eligibility Center form if you hope to play Division I or II sports. This form cannot be mailed until you finish your sixth semester of high school.

Senior Year

Apply to colleges. Make decisions. Finish high school with pride in yourself and your accomplishments.

August/September

- Make sure you have all applications, websites and/or Common Application (www. commonapp.org) required for college admission and financial aid. Write, phone, or use the Internet to request missing information.

- Check on application and financial aid deadlines for the schools to which you plan to apply. They may vary, and it is essential to meet all deadlines!

- Meet with your counselor to be sure your list includes colleges appropriate to your academic and personal record. Review your transcript and co-curricular records with your school counselor to ensure their accuracy.

- Register for the October/November SAT Reasoning Test and/or SAT Subject Tests, and/or September/October ACT.

- If the colleges require recommendations, ask the appropriate people to write on your behalf. At least three weeks before the due date, ask your counselor and teachers, employers, or coaches to write letters of recommendation. Provide recommendation forms, any special instructions, and a stamped, addressed business envelope to the people writing your recommendations. Be thoughtful! Write thank you notes to those who write recommendations, and keep them informed of your decisions. Check with them regularly so you can be sure the deed was done!

- Plan visits to colleges and set up interviews if you didn't get to them during the summer or if you want to return to a campus for a second time. Read bulletin boards and the college newspapers. Talk with current students and professors. Sit in classes, eat in the dining hall, and don't just settle for the official tour—branch out on your own, too.

October

- Attend a regional college fair to investigate further those colleges to which you will probably apply. Go to College Fairs on NACAC's website (www.nacacnet.org) to view the schedule for NACAC's National College Fairs and the Performing and Visual Arts College Fairs.

- Mail /submit electronic applications in time to reach the colleges by their deadlines. Check with your counselor to make sure your transcript and test scores have been or will be sent to the colleges to which you are applying.

- If applying for early decision or early action, send in your application now. Also prepare applications for back-up schools. Remember, if you are accepted under the early decision option, you are expected to enroll at that college and to withdraw all other applications. Submit financial aid information if requested from early decision/action candidates.

- Register for the December/January SAT Reasoning Test and/or SAT Subject Tests, or December ACT if you have not completed the required tests or if you are not happy with your previous test scores and think you can do better.

- Have official test scores sent by the testing agency to colleges on your list.

November

- Take the ACT and/or SAT Reasoning Test or SAT Subject Tests if appropriate. Don't forget to have test scores sent to colleges on your list.

- Be sure your first quarter grades are good.

- Continue completing applications to colleges. Make copies of all applications before mailing the applications.

- If you need financial aid, obtain a (Free Application for Federal Student Aid (FAFSA) from www.fafsa.ed.gov. Check to see if the colleges to which you are applying require any other financial aid form. Register for the College Scholarship Service (CSS) Profile if required and obtain the college's own financial aid forms, if available.

- Keep all records, test score reports and copies of applications for admission and financial aid. Do not throw anything away until at least the end of your first year in college. Having detailed records will save you time and effort, should anything be lost, or should you decide to apply in the future to other colleges and scholarship programs.

December

- Have official test scores sent to the colleges on your list if you have not done so.

- Consult your counselor again to review your final list of colleges. Consult your checklists to make sure you include everything required in the envelopes. It is a good idea to make copies of everything before you drop those envelopes in the mail. If for some reason your application gets lost, you will have a back-up copy. File your last college application.

- If you applied for early decision, you should have an answer by December 20th. If you are accepted, follow the instructions for admitted students. If the decision is deferred until spring or you are denied, submit applications now to other colleges.

- To get ready to submit your FAFSA on line in January, apply for your Personal Information Number (PIN) at www.fafsa.ed.gov.

January

- Keep working in your classes! Grades and courses continue to count throughout the senior year.

- Request that your counselor send the transcript of your first semester grades to the colleges to which you applied.

- Parents and students, complete your income tax forms as soon as possible. You will need those figures to fill out the FAFSA. Submit your FAFSA on-line as quickly as possible after January 1. Check to make sure your colleges and state do not require any other financial aid forms. If they do, consult your guidance counselor or contact the college's financial aid office.

February

- Remember to monitor your applications to be sure that all materials are sent and received on time and that they are complete. Stay on top of things and don't procrastinate; you can ruin your chances for admission by missing a deadline.

- If you submitted a FAFSA, you should receive your Student Aid Report (SAR) within 2 weeks after submitting the FAFSA online. Review the SAR carefully and check for any inaccuracies. If necessary, correct any items on the SAR and return it to the FAFSA processor. (If a college transmitted your data directly, notify the college of any change.)

- If you have questions or concerns, contact the Federal Student Aid Information Center at (319) 337-5665. To identify you, the representative will need your name, social security number, address, and date of birth, exactly as they were written on your FAFSA.

- Complete scholarship applications. You may be eligible for more scholarships than you think, so apply for as many as you can.

- Enjoy your final year in high school, but don't catch senioritis!

March

- Stay focused and keep studying—only a couple more months to go!

April

- Some colleges do not have application deadlines; they admit students on a continuous basis, in what is called "rolling admissions." Do not take rolling admission applications for granted. These schools may reach their maximum class size quickly—the earlier you apply, the more availability there may be.

- Review your college acceptances and financial aid awards. Be sure to compare financial aid packages in your decision-making process. If you are positive you will not enroll at one or more of the colleges that accepted you, please notify those colleges that you have selected another school. Keeping colleges abreast of your plans might enable those colleges to admit someone else. If you know which college you will attend, send your tuition deposit and follow all other instructions for admitted students. You must decide which offer of admission to accept by May 1st (postmark date).

May

- By May 1st, send in your tuition deposit to the one college that you have decided to attend. Notify the other colleges that accepted you that you have selected another college.

- BE PROUD—you have completed a difficult task.

- If your first-choice college places you on its waiting list, do not lose all hope. Some students on waiting lists are admitted. Talk with your counselor, and contact the college to indicate that you are still very interested (if you really are). Keep the college updated on your activities.

- Take Advanced Placement examinations, if appropriate, and request that your AP scores be sent to the college you will attend.

June

- Request that your counselor send your final transcript to the college you will attend. Notify the college of any private scholarships or grants you will be receiving.

- Know the due dates for the payment for tuition, room and board, meal plans, etc. If necessary, ask the financial aid office about a possible payment plan that will allow for you to pay in installments.

- Congratulations, you've made it through high school! Enjoy your graduation and look forward to college.

July

- Look for information in the mail from the college about housing, roommate(s), orientation, course selection, etc. Respond promptly to all requests from the college.

August–September

- Ease the transition into college. Accept the fact that you'll be in charge of your academic and personal life. What you do, when you do it and how things get done will be up to you. You'll have new responsibilities and challenges. Think about budgeting your time and establishing priorities. Take charge of the changes that lie ahead, and eliminate or minimize pressures. Go forth with confidence and enthusiasm, willingness to adapt, and determination to succeed academically and personally.

- Pack for college. Don't forget to include things that remind you of friends and family. Be prepared for the new opportunities and challenges. Have a great freshman year!

Reprinted from NACAC's PACT Guide, Revised, March 2005. The National Association for College Admission Counseling.

Reprinted with permission. Copyright 2008, National Association for College Admission Counseling.

SECTION 2:
Writing a "WOW!" Application Essay

Debbie E. Merion, MFA, MSW

How Are Students Puzzled by the College Application Essay?

Most colleges require one or more personal essays as part of their application. Students are puzzled about this for a number of reasons. They are not sure of the purpose of the essay, they don't know what to write, and they often don't know a process for how to write a winning essay. Because students may feel puzzled and overwhelmed, they may procrastinate and worry about this part of their application. Reading this chapter will help.

A college application essay is not the same type of essay that your English teachers have been talking about for years.

When it comes to essay structure, a five paragraph essay is not required. The major structure is this: make sure that your essay answers the question and sticks to the word length. When no word length is given, it is best to not exceed 500 words. Draw in your reader with details, and keep them compelled to read to the end with a your unique experiences and reflections.

Your challenge is to craft a compelling personal essay in your own voice to interest and excite a busy college admissions officer who has never met you.

One applicant explained it like this: "High school essays are about what we know. College application essays are about who we are." She was right. Colleges want to know more about you than simply whether you can get an "A" on your physics test. They often have to choose between many students who can get an "A."

Keep in mind that colleges are looking for the more impressive student. They read what you say in your essay and they read between the lines. They choose the student they understand, respect and like, the one who shows more maturity, self-insight, initiative, intellectual curiosity, passion, creativity, focus, and/or drive. They choose the student who they believe will fit into their college, contribute, be successful, and graduate. So the goal is to portray yourself in your essay in a positive, authentic, and memorable way.

Does My Essay Make a Difference in Getting Admitted?

College admissions officers read your essay to learn about your strengths and attitudes in your own unique voice. You're more than your name, activities, AP classes and numbers—a 3.9 GPA, a 22 ACT, a 1650 SAT score.

Imagine you are a college admissions officer drinking a cup of coffee to get through 20 applications this day. So many GPAs and advanced placement classes are the same, transcript after transcript. Then you get to the essay. Ah, the essay is a breath of fresh air, a creative commercial, something to sink your teeth into and a way to get to know a student.

An admissions officer will think about you after he reads your transcript and the application, to decide whether to offer you admission. He'll picture you with images from the essay. MORAL: Paint positive, strong images to be remembered by! He might think of you as "the Iowa kid who loves reading Shakespeare at night with a flashlight," or "the Ann Arbor Pioneer student who is proud to be a Republican in a Democratic town," or "the tall African-American girl who wants to be a lawyer, not play basketball with her friends."

Can your essay make a difference in you being admitted? Yes, it can. In particular, smaller schools usually weight essays more heavily than larger schools. Here are some voices on this subject from College Essays that Made a Difference:

"An essay can have significant impact on the decision."

–*Parke Muth, Senior Assistant Dean of Admissions at University of Virginia*

"If an essay is poorly written, does not address the assigned topic, or includes inappropriate content, it is unlikely the applicant will be considered for admission."

–*Duncan Murdoch, Dean of Admission at Franklin W. Olin College of Engineering*

"There are essays that are compelling, that make a difference. A great essay can carry the student. A poor essay might do the opposite."

–*John Latting, Director of Admissions at Johns Hopkins University*

What is a Quick Overview of How to Write a Winning Essay?

Puzzlement and procrastination rarely get results. A pithy, clever saying is: "If you fail to plan, you plan to fail." Travel one step at a time on a clear path ahead of you. This chapter outlines that path and walks along with you. There are five steps and five tips to help you.

Five steps for writing a winning essay:

1) Organize the essay questions and application deadlines from all the schools that interest you onto one list. These are schools that you may have visited, read about, and heard about from others.

2) Stir up your thoughts and emotions.

3) Choose a topic that you want to write about and will reflect well on you.

4) Write it like you're telling a true story.

5) Edit frequently and carefully.

What Is My Essay Voice and How Do I Find It?

"We are looking for students who write coherent, thoughtful, carefully organized, mechanically sound, and hopefully imaginative prose. Sometimes that's flashy, and sometimes it is not.… We try and find some way to say to young people, 'Write in your own voice.'"

– *The Dean of Admissions at Bates College, in* Essays that Worked for College Applications

What is your writing voice? Your voice is a natural part of you. It's different from everyone else's. It's in the words you choose and the way you arrange them into sentences and paragraphs to express who you are inside. Are you exuberant and exploring? Are you deep and directed? Do you have a photographic memory? Are you the "underdog" who won't stop trying until you succeed?

You can't hide those qualities from emerging in your writing voice, any more than you can hide the sound of sadness in your speaking voice when you've just heard bad news. Your writing voice in a great college essay will sound very similar to your speaking voice when you're feeling your most passionate and engaged and thoughtful—without, of course, the fill-in words we all use when we speak: "um" "like," "you know."

How do you find your essay voice? Here are four easy techniques:

- **Write Quickly, Don't Judge:** Write some initial thoughts quickly like an artist sketching. "Feel free to write the worst junk in America," says master writing teacher and author Natalie Goldberg. Turning down the pressure on yourself to write your best paradoxically helps fresh, vivid thoughts to flow onto paper.

- **Show, Don't Tell:** Use detailed, strong sensory images. If you're telling a ski story, help us see the blinding powdery flakes of snow and feel the stinging cold on your wrists when you fall and your sense of relief as your father picks you up and sends you down the slope again.

- **Be Enthusiastic and Passionate!** Write about what you care about and how you've taken the initiative to explore your passion.

- **Write About What's Happening Outside of You and Inside of You:** Take time to describe exactly what happened outside of you (events that happened or where you took initiative) and inside of you (thoughts and feelings about the events).

Here are some examples of different ways you can say the same thing:

A sample essay line	Comments on using this line
1. I am confident.	Even if you are confident, just saying that you are isn't a good idea. It's your own self-judgement. You need information to back it up. It's better to let a reader surmise you're confident from your story. Show, don't tell.
2. I smile at people.	This is better, because it says something about your behavior. But the smile is still not in context...When do you smile and why?
3. I smile at people when I pass them in the hallways.	This is better than #2 because it provides a memorable image. Just this one sentence pinpoints you as unique—how many students do you know who smile at people in the hall when they're busy passing between classes?
4. I smile at people when I pass them in the hallways. Sometimes they even smile back, and I wonder, "Will we become friends?" Because I know that's one way that friendships start.	This is the best alternative. You are drawing a strong image for the reader. There's a connection between an experience and your thoughts reflecting on the experience. You are showing your inner strength because your smile is not dependent on others' reactions. Readers of these sentences may read between the lines and see you as confident, friendly, risk-taking for a positive goal (not afraid to get shot down by unrequited smiles), self-aware (knowing why she does what she does), and as a person with a vision: all characteristics of leaders.

What Does the Admissions Officer Want to Know About Me?

The best essay leaves the reader excited about you as a prospective student in his or her school.

The college admissions officer reads your essay to visualize you:

- Attending that school
- Contributing positively in class and in the college community
- Graduating with a good GPA in approximately 4 years

They are looking for students who show maturity, self-insight, initiative, intellectual curiosity, passion, creativity, focus, and/or drive.

You are an expert on you. The college admissions officer is an expert on his or her college environment. Your job is to convince him or her that you fit into his or her environment.

Ask yourself these questions: How and why would I fit in or be an asset on the campus? How would my contributions be unique—for example, different from my best friends? Talk to people, call the school, and read about the institution on the web and in its written materials. Visit the school if you can, so you can see what the college admissions officer sees every day. Then you can build your understanding into your essay.

What are the Characteristics of the Most Highly-Competitive Students?

Colleges cannot accept all qualified applicants. A strong essay emphasizing the following qualities can help you stand out amonst your peers.

Anagram to remember: GET In Lead

- **G**rowth potential or evidence in areas of interest
- **E**nthusiastic (AKA passionate)
- **T**alented
- (show) **IN**itiative
- (demonstrate) **LEAD**ership

How Do I Get Started?

Get Organized

Learn:

- The exact essay questions for the schools you are interested in. Note that not all colleges require essays.
- Whether the schools you are interested in take the Common Application (www.commonapp.org). You can use that application for over 300 schools.
- Application deadlines.

Decide:

- Where the folders with your applications and college information booklets will live in your house (kitchen shelf? A box in your bedroom?) Keep a blank notebook with it for writing. Jot down notes in the notebook whenever they come to you...any idea, any time, day or night.

- Where the folders with your virtual applications and college information will live on your computer.

Here is a sample chart you can use to help yourself get organized. If you are using your computer to maintain this chart, set up your page using landscape format to get the widest area.

Colleges you are considering (sample list below)	Deadline for Application	Exact essay questions	Do they take the common application? yes/no	Ranking of school by your interest	Ranking of school by deadline
University of Michigan					
UCLA					
Denison University					
Florida State University					

Common Application Essay Questions

Here are some recent common application (www.commonapp.org) essay questions. Only one common app essay is required (250 word minimum):

1. Some students have a background, identity, interest, or talent that is so meaningful they believe their application would be incomplete without it. If this sounds like you, then please share your story.

2. The lessons we take from failure can be fundamental to later success. Recount an incident or time when you experienced failure. How did it affect you, and what did you learn from the experience?

3. Reflect on a time when you challenged a belief or idea. What prompted you to act? Would you make the same decision again?

4. Describe a problem you've solved or a problem you'd like to solve. It can be an intellectual challenge, a research query, an ethical dilemma-anything that is of personal importance, no matter the scale. Explain its significance to you and what steps you took or could be taken to identify a solution.

5. Discuss an accomplishment or event, formal or informal, that marked your transition from childhood to adulthood within your culture, community, or family.

What are Some Pre-Writing Activities?

Some people feel paralyzed when they think of writing the essay, so let's start with some easy tasks for prewriting: stir up your thoughts and memories, identify your strongest qualities, describe a situation that shows those qualities, and use one of your ideas a writing prompt. *Additional activities are in Appendix II.*

Stir Up Your Thoughts and Emotions

Set the timer for one minute and write the first ideas that come into your head.

Three ways I'm different from my friends

    1

    2

    3

Three subjects I could talk about for an hour

    1

    2

    3

Three reasons my friends, teachers, and coaches respect and value my presence

    1

    2

    3

Circle Your Five Strongest Qualities

Action-oriented	Energetic	Masterful	Risk-taker
Aware	Flexible	Motivated	Sensitive
Assertive	Friendly	Open-minded	Strong
Careful	Goal-oriented	Organized	Supportive
Caring	Hardworking	Passionate	Tactful
Competent	Helpful	Persistent	Thorough
Considerate	Honest	Persuasive	Tolerant
Creative	Humorous	Poised	Trustworthy
Curious	Imaginative	Political	Warm
Decisive	Intellectual	Precise	Willing
Dedicated	Intelligent	Quick	Worldly
Determined	Intense	Resilient	*(add others)*
Diligent	Intuitive	Responsible	_____
Easygoing	Inquisitive	Results-oriented	_____
Efficient	Loyal	Rigid	_____

Describe Two Situations About Two of the Qualities

Very briefly describe a situation that occurred in the last six months where you acted out one of your strongest qualities (e.g. helping your grandparent move, tutoring at orchestra camp).

Now, can you remember a time when you didn't have one of your strong qualities? Why did you change? How did it happen? How are you different now?

Use One of Your Ideas as a Writing Prompt

Now that you've filled in the blanks, we're going to use one of your ideas as a prompt for some initial writing, to stir up your thoughts and memories some more. But we're going to try a new way to write—writing quickly and without self-judgment ("it's great," "it's terrible") so that your words will flow easily onto the page. Here are the rules:

a.   Set a timer for 10 minutes.

b.   Select a topic from your fill-in blanks above that you feel drawn to.

c.   After you start the timer, keep your hand moving and don't cross out.

d.   Don't worry about spelling, punctuation, grammar.

e.   Don't judge what you write. Master writing teacher Natalie Goldberg says, "Feel free to write the worst junk in America."

The writing that you produce from writing practice will not be your essay. However, it will:

- Guide you in making a choice about your topic. (Read more about making a choice in the next question.)

- Get some words on the page so you can get past any fear that the essay won't get done.

- Get you started thinking more about yourself. As you write you will remember more.

"I write entirely to find out what I'm thinking, what I'm looking at, what I see and what it means."

—Joan Didion, author of *The Year of Magical Thinking*

How Do I Pick the Best Topic for My Essay?

"There are terrible essays on wonderful topics and wonderful essays on very ordinary topics. The topic itself does not make the essay."

–Margit Dahl, Dean of Undergraduate Admissions at Yale,
in *College Essays that Made a Difference* by the Princeton Review, 2012

To pick the best topic for you, write about what you care about and what you have done about it.

Write about what you feel passionate about—something positive. If you feel great about what you're writing about, that will transfer to your voice. The reader will feel your enthusiasm through the page. Also, people are usually knowledgeable about what they love—this might be one of the things you said you could talk about for an hour.

Obviously there are limits here. It will be difficult to write a winning essay about how much you love to party or watch "Sex and the City" reruns. And you may feel very passionate about your grandmother who passed away, but can you write about her in a story that will be enjoyable to read, not sad and depressing, and show something about you? Your passion can be a person, a place, an activity, a book, an idea.

You might want to bounce your ideas off of someone else. This person can ask: Why do you love this? What have you done about it? Have your experiences with this person or thing changed you? Is this a unique idea? Is there an interesting story or anecdote that you can tell that can make this idea the basis of a unique essay?

Suppose you want to write about hockey because you're passionate about it and you spend a lot of time with it. But, you think, "All my friends love hockey too, so how unique is that?" You're right and you're wrong. Sports essays are common. But if you're committed to it, and can't think of an alternative, make your sports essay your own. Make your essay bigger than the ball skills, the score of the game, the winning and the losing. Talk about why you chose that sport, what it meant to you, how it changed you. Provide details to the college admissions officer who is reading the essay. Tell a story about you that no one else can tell.

Again, there are limits here. How offbeat is OK?

If you're uncomfortable with an idea for any reason, or an adult is, accept the evaluation and pick another topic.

Here are some popular categories for essays:

A Moral Dilemma	**A Significant Experience**
About the College Application Process	**Academics**
Activity and Sports Essays	**Coming to America**
Counseling and Community Service	**Home**
Humor	**Offbeat Essays**
Personal Growth	**Plants and Animals**
Politics and Religion	**Realization Essays**
Relationships and Family	**Self-Description**
Taking a Year Off	**The Arts**
Why I love First Choice U	**Work Experience including Camp**

Do I Need to Write a Five Paragraph Essay?

A standard five-paragraph essay is usually not called for, though the actual structure of the essay you write depends on who you are and what question you are answering.

Your college essay is about who you are: high school essays are usually about what you know.

All college essays are creative nonfiction, therefore there is a wider variety of structure that can be included. One way is to tell a true story, usually from your point of view as the main character. You tell your story by describing your experiences and your thoughts and feelings. You may also use dialogue. Quotations are great, but make sure they are punctuated correctly.

> *"We're right here, but we should've hit the Appalachian Trail back there," I said matter-of-factly. "Well, what are we going to do!?" said Laurie, searching my face for an answer.*

Follow These Steps When Creating Your Essay Structure

Always write the exact essay question at the top of the page. Copy and paste it from the online application.

- The opening sentences are like the front door. They should be inviting, and give people a taste of what is to come. How excited would you be about visiting someone with a dingy grey door and a dirty, stuck doorknob? Write opening sentences that are strong, catchy, descriptive, or intriguing.

- Once readers are past the front door, it's your job to give them a tour to help them get to know your experiences, thoughts and emotions, and to keep them engaged and moving and impressed with the images they see and the words they hear.

- The closing sentences provide a positive, unique, thought-provoking, memorable ending that reinforces your story and its main points.

How Long Should an Essay Be?

Read the application instructions carefully when you organize your essay questions. Some college applications specify a minimum length, some specify a maximum, and some specify approximate lengths.

If the specifications don't specify a maximum, try to keep your essay within 300 and 600 words in length. Most essays, columns or editorials you see printed in a newspaper or magazine are within this range. Shorter essays are often stronger: repetition is eliminated. Because they take less time to complete, readers have the time to read them twice.

Because it is often easier to write something long than to write something short, students sometimes try to find wiggle room in the rules, like driving through a traffic light when it has just turned red. This is where you need to use good judgment.

Every word over the word limit increases the risk of a "thumbs down" because the reader loses interest, can't find the main point, or is confused about facts or descriptions.

Readers always appreciate conciseness:

> *"A sentence should contain no unnecessary words for the same reason that a machine should have no unnecessary parts."*

> —William Strunk, Jr., *The Elements of Style, 1959*

Here are some tips for keeping your essay within the limit:

1) Write the essay early enough so that you can edit it five to ten times, with a day or two separating each reading. Each time you read the essay, you'll see words to cut. Does a sentence bore you? Cut it! Are you repeating yourself? Cut!

2) Make precise word choices. For example, substitute "remove" for "take off," or "prepare" for "get ready."

3) Aim for a first draft word length that is ¾ the length of the required essay. That leaves you room to add names, places, colors, dialogue, adjectives, transitions, and reflections during the editing stage.

How Can I Avoid Sounding Boastful?

Paint word pictures. Use quantifying (for example, "two years") or factually descriptive words (for example, "cat biology lab") rather than adjectives such as "top" or "best." Compare:

"Last year I got a job in the top lab on campus."

To the less boastful and more informative:

"During my junior year I worked as a lab tech in the University of Michigan's cat biology lab, which currently has two 5-year NIH grants."

Here are some more ways to impress others without sounding boastful. Describe:

- What you thought or felt in a situation. *"I told myself that I knew I could make the soccer team if I focused on it completely. Every day I visualized myself scoring a goal in our school uniform."*

- Exactly what you did in a situation. For example, one student described his wet, sweaty labor when he traveled to New Orleans to help the victims of Hurricane Katrina, and how the favorite jeans he wore now look—blotchy with brown and grey stains that won't come out in the wash.

- What you said, when talking with others about a situation.

- A physical description of yourself in a situation.

- How others have role modeled behavior for you that you try to follow. *"My grandmother taught me to knit when I was eight. The red wool kept falling off the needles, but night after night, stitch after stitch, she patiently helped me make my first scarf—a birthday gift for my mom."*

- What others have said to you or about you. For example, *"My instructor asked me to teach the beginning dance class when I was twelve."*

Use Memorable Phrases

You can avoid being boastful but still be memorable in a positive way by using certain phrases:

- **Pictures and Metaphors**—Readers form images in their minds of the situations and people you describe in your essay. "I think of myself as a sneaker" was a metaphor used as a theme in a college essay that remained memorable over the years to one college admissions counselor. Make sure that a metaphor is explained and fits well for the idea you want to communicate.

- **Names**—names of people, places, books.

- **Sensory details**—colors, smells, sounds, textures, tastes.

- **Nouns**—Interesting things, things that mean something to you. For example, your piano, your ice skates, your grandfather's watch.

- **Dialogue**—Phrases said that are pithy, wise, honest, funny, or perfect for the moment and the speaker.

- **Emotions**—Either described in the essay, or aroused in the readers.

- **Surprises**—Story surprises can delight us, just like surprise parties and gift surprises do.

- **Numbers and values**—For example, the above list provided eight ways to make your essay memorable.

How Can I Write About a Problem?

Occasionally a high school counselor will recommend that you consider writing about a problem that has affected your grades or your test scores in your essay. You can talk about problems but still be positive about yourself, not defensive.

- Compare and contrast the problem with something that's not a problem for you. *"It was a relief to learn I had a natural knack for running and I could excel in that area, because some subjects in school, like reading and writing, had always been difficult for me. Later I found out I had dyslexia."*

- Mention how you've dealt with the problem and overcome it. *"I learned study skills to handle my dyslexia. Because I know I need extra time, I always carry my calendar with me and schedule my homework when I get the assignment."*

- Say how lessons you've learned from overcoming this problem have helped you to deal with others. *"When my mother died, I learned to be more independent. I made my own doctor's appointments, unlike my friends. So when my dad told me we had to move, although it was upsetting to me, I knew I had the skills to help take care of myself, wherever we ended up."*

- Talk about how others have role modeled or taught you that you can overcome this problem. *"My parents never went to college, but when my sister went to Eastern Michigan, I realized I could go to college too. I suddenly felt relieved that I wouldn't have to work on the line at Chrysler, like my dad, or in Office Max, like my mom."*

What are the Most Common Essay Mistakes?

A simple typo or grammatical error in an interesting, compelling, informative essay can be as much as a turnoff to a college admissions officer as spinach in your teeth would be on a hot date. Some admissions officers see a single grammatical error as a "red flag" and a reason to reject your application. Look up any grammatical questions you have in your high school grammar book.

But grammar isn't everything. Once I had a student present me with the worst essay I'd ever read. He retold his favorite family stories that he thought were funny but that sounded so cruel they made me cringe. I felt like I was talking to the son in the Addams Family TV show. He asked about his essay, *"Is it grammatically correct?"* I had to say it was. But that didn't make it a great or even good essay. I discussed with him how to strengthen the content.

Here are the ten most common mistakes:

- Writing that is so general the reader learns little about you. Be specific. Include sensory deal (smells, sounds, colors, images) and names, places and dates. Don't say "I love books." Say, "I read novels, but my favorite has always been Huckleberry Finn—I read it every year around my birthday."

- Essays without self-reflection. Self-reflection means you've thought about and commented on your own behavior. Ask yourself: Why did I do that? How did a situation change me, if at all? How did I take initiative?

- Not writing in your own voice. Your written words should sound similar to your spoken words. See the thoughts earlier in this section on finding your voice.

- Cramming the essay full of qualifications instead of having a central idea and focus.

- Spending two long describing experiences that occurred before a major change in your life. Use this formula: 1/3 essay content before change, 2/3 essay content to explain the reason for and results of the change.

- Essays that lose a reader's interest because they are too long (over 600 words) or repetitive.

- Saying "you" or "us" when you mean "I."

- Not including the writing prompt/question at the top of the page.

- Not being specific about why a school appeals to you. This is where a visit and research can be helpful. Also, when you customize the essay for a school, triple check that you have the correct school name in the essay.

- A weak first sentence that doesn't hook the reader with your story. A weak ending sentence instead of one that leaves the reader satisfied, interested, smiling.

Avoid Red-Flag Essay Problems

- Start writing your essay early. Start before September of your senior year—spring of your junior year is best—so you have plenty of time to edit.

- Read your essay over and over out loud, from paper, on different days. Let it "marinate" in between readings.

- Use the three levels of edits described below.

How Should I Edit?

Here are three levels of editing, moving from larger, structural issues to smaller details. In general, try to complete one level of editing before you move on to the next one.

1. **The first level of editing: Smooth out the major issues.**

   • Make sure your essay answers the entire question by reading it over again from the top of the page.

   • Ask yourself, "What does the reader learn about me from this?"

   • Add detail and reflections wherever possible.

   • Make sure the essay fits the school. Know exactly what appeals to you about that school.

   • Pay special attention to the first and last sentences.

2. **The second level of editing: Print it out and read aloud to yourself or a listener.**

   • Pick someone you trust for feedback.

   • Give your listener a few brief instructions/questions, such as "What did you learn about me from reading this? What are the best parts? Are my sentences too choppy or too long? Do you have any questions about any section?"

3. **The third level of editing: Proofreading.**

   • Give yourself some time between the edits to give yourself perspective or be more alert when you are editing.

   • Print and read out loud or have someone else read it to you, listening for awkward phrasing and inconsistency.

   • Make sure each sentence and paragraph follows logically and smoothly from the one before. (Transition words include: since, before, though, finally, in spite of, therefore.)

   • Use a spell checker and grammar checker.

4. **Before you press SEND, ask yourself:**

   • Did I answer the question?

   • What will the reader learn about me from reading this essay?

   • Have I reflected on my experiences to show my understanding of who I am?

   • Have I read the essay over, out loud, from paper?

   • Did I run the spell checker and grammar checker and carefully read to find the errors these checkers can't find?

   • Is the name of the school correct in the essay?

Repeat the above editing levels until you're confident additional editing won't help. Give the same scrutiny to the rest of your application, cross your fingers and press SEND!

> *"If a student reads his application before mailing it and can say 'this sounds like me,' then he's probably written the best essay possible."*

> —*Essays that Worked for College Applications,*
> by Boykin Curry, Brian Kasbar, and Emily Angel Baer

What Can I Do to Reduce the Stress in Writing Essays?

The best way to reduce the stress related to writing the college essay is:

1) **Start early.** Begin during the spring and summer before your senior year. This gives you plenty of time to think, ask questions and let your essay "marinate." Research online, talk with people and visit schools to help you with content ideas.

2) **Get organized** so you have your application dates and application in one place. Set up a calendar with all of your dates and deadlines.

3) **Write anything** you can think of for your essay in a single notebook. Write lists, brainstorms, free writes, memories, and drafts.

4) **Talk to people** about your essay thoughts and questions. Talk with college counselors at the school you're interested in applying to, your high school college counselor, a parent, teacher, or coach.

5) **If you get behind, don't panic.** The key is to start as soon as possible, work on your essay every day, and allot time on your calendar for writing. Be strict with yourself. Keep dates with yourself; then reward yourself when you meet the commitment.

What Kind of Help Can I Ask for From My Parents and Other Adults?

Here are some ways that families and adults can offer to support students writing their college essays but still maintain the boundary that students must write the essay themselves.

Families – Sit down together before the student starts the essay process and talk. Really! It can be that simple. Prior to writing, students think about the essay questions and topics, and ponder their own possible answers. Parents and other family members may remember situations illustrating a student's strengths that students may have forgotten. Beside helping with ideas, families can support the student emotionally, organizationally, and help a student visit colleges. Near the end of the process, parents can help with proofreading if asked.

> *"I would think it foolish of a student not to have an essay proofed for spelling, grammar and syntax by someone competent to do so."*
>
> – Jeffrey Brenzel from Yale, in *The New York Times Magazine*, May 20, 2007

College counselors in the college and in high school provide the big picture about the type of student a school is seeking.

English teachers and writers can offer insight into how a student can strengthen his or her essay to make the writing more compelling and error-free. English teachers can recreate a college essay experience in class by assigning a college essay for a writing assignment.

Low-cost assistance, including classes – Many free and low-cost talks are sponsored by the library, teen organizations, writing organizations, and the school system. Start with your college counselor, English teacher, or librarian when seeking assistance. Ask about local essay writing classes and professionals. Read sample essays on your own. See the biography at the end of this book.

College consultants and writing coaches can reduce the stress for parents. Such professionals help by creating writing process structure via meetings, writing exercises and goals. They offer experience in bringing out a student's unique voice and strengths. They also offer a knowledgeable and fresh viewpoint, similar to that of a college admissions officer.

The best coaches and consultants:

- Help students to understand the criteria for a winning college essay, so that they can learn to evaluate their essays knowledgeably.

- Are positive and encouraging. Even the weakest essay can be strengthened if a student understands what needs to be done and is willing to do the work.

- Enjoy working with students and respect their individual abilities.

- Listen to students read their essays out loud as much as possible before the final draft.

- Ask thought provoking questions and react honestly to what they hear. "This is what I learned from you from hearing your essay." Or "This part confused me. Why did you say that?" The explanation from the student may then need to be included in the essay. It's like an explanation after a quotation in an analytic essay.

- Do not write on the essay—that's the student's job. The student decides the changes to make, and makes them.

"I think it's perfectly all right for a parent or friend to read the essay, but they shouldn't do it with a red pen in hand."

–Margit A. Dahl from Yale, in College *Essays that Made a Difference*

Would It Help to Write an Essay If It's Optional?

The more time a college officer spends thinking about you, the better it is for you. He may never have met you, but he can get to know you before you even apply by your handwriting, your promptness, your questions, your interests, your campus visit, and your high school counselor. The optional essay is one more opportunity for the college officer to know who you are and discover that you would be a worthy addition to his institution—which means, in general, if you can write an appealing optional essay with new information that a school can't find out in other ways, write it. If you are pressed for time or feel like you only have one decent essay in you, don't do it.

What Are 10 Tips for Writing a "Wow" Essay?

Remember these key points about the stages in the essay writing process:

1. Get organized. Write a short-list of schools that you want to apply to. These are schools that you may have visited, read about, heard about from others. Look up their applications and gather the essay questions and application deadlines in one place.

2. Stir up your thoughts and emotions.

3. Choose a topic using good judgment.

4. Write it like you're telling a creative nonfiction story.

5. Edit frequently and carefully using the three levels of editing. Listen to your own writing when you read the essay out loud, as well as your own good judgment, and the judgment and advice of knowledgeable adults. Remember to ask, "What does the reader learn about me from reading this essay?"

    As you go through the process, remember to:

6. Quiet your editor when creating. Tell your judgmental editor to "be quiet now" while you are stirring up your thoughts and emotions and writing. Invite your editor back to the process when you choose a topic and edit.

7. Have balance. Take time to recall exactly what happened inside of you (thoughts and feelings) and outside of you (events that happened or where you took initiative).

8. Be enthusiastic and passionate! Write about something you really care about. Link your current activities and lifestyle with both your past and your vision of your future.

9. Make your essay positive and memorable by showing your strengths with detailed, strong sensory images that show rather than tell. Describe situations you've experienced and reflect on them.

10. Customize. Make sure the essay fits the question, the school and your vision of how this is the right school for you.

Conclusion

Remember your college essays as a hologram of your best moments as a high school senior. Keep writing, keep learning, and ENJOY COLLEGE!!!

Essay Writing Schedule

Sophomore and Junior Years

Research colleges you are interested in. If you are able to visit the school, look over its application's essay questions before the visit. This research will help you think about the essay.

Summer Between Junior and Senior Year

Many students want to have their essay complete by the time they start school in September, because they get busy with homework and activities. Here is a schedule for taking your time with your essays over the summer or, if you prefer, any eight-week block that allows you to meet your application deadlines.

Week 1 (July before Senior Year)

Print out the essay questions of all the colleges you're considering applying to, including the common application questions. Read them over and put them in a binder. Get a writing notebook/journal or set up a file on your computer. Decide where this information will live in your house (which shelf or drawer) and make a pact with yourself to always put it back there.

Leave the essay questions in a place where you can read them over each day and think about them, while you're shopping, driving, during dinner. Talk about them with your parents.

If the essay questions are multiple choice, circle any that seem like they might be the choice you'd pick to write about. No formal writing yet—just thinking, with some rough ideas jotted down in your notebook if something comes to you.

Week 2

Write lists and do writing practice as described in this chapter, to stir up your thoughts and memories.

Week 3

Decide on a topic using good judgment. Talk about it with others.

Week 4 (August before Senior Year)

Write your thoughts in idea form. At this point it is too early to even call this a first draft. Set a timer for 10 minutes each day and just write on the topic.

Week 5

Read over everything you wrote last week, and then try to remember which parts you liked best. Which phrases and sections were unique or exciting? Circle them, and delete everything else. Work on organizing them into a draft that tells a true story about you and your strengths.

Week 6

Talk with people about your draft. Read your essay out loud to a teacher, a counselor, a parent, a writing coach. It's just a draft; you have nothing to lose! Tell your listener the kind of feedback you need to hear. "Just tell me what you've learned about me from reading this." Or "What do you think about this topic? What sounds interesting about what I said?"

Week 7

Edit, edit, edit. Edit every day, even if it is 10 minutes each day.

Week 8

Edit more. Some students ask others to read what they've written to help spot typos. If the rest of the application is all together, press SEND at the end of the week.

Of course, you don't have to use an eight-week schedule. If you can sit down and write your 250-word essay in an hour, do it! That will catapult you to week 6. If you want to start in February of your junior year, stretch out the eight-week essay schedule. Some students do this. By the time September of senior year rolls around, their essays are complete and they can devote full time to their school and sports and other activities during that busy senior fall.

SECTION 3:
Those Nerve-Wracking ACT/SAT Tests

Geraldine Markel, PhD

How are Students Puzzled by the ACT/SAT?

Joan, a junior, yells at her parents, "All you do is nag, nag, and nag! I don't have time to study for all this stuff! I get home late from swim practice and need to do my homework. I'm nervous enough about the ACT and now you're bugging me about AP courses. Leave me alone!"

Chaos reigns in Joan's home. She's upset, her parents are puzzled, and the chances that she'll do her best on those nerve-wracking college admissions tests dwindle as each month marches by. Overwhelmed, Joan avoids planning and preparing—and shuts down.

Phil, another junior at the same school, feels more control. He talks with his parents: "I can't believe how bad I did on the PSAT. My reading was all right, but my math sucks. My friend has a tutor. Maybe I could go to the same one."

Control is emerging for Phil and his family. He reviews his PSAT results and identifies a skill area to improve and a way to improve it. He is involved and motivated. He knows that he is doing something to help himself. Students who know where they stand and how they can improve are less likely to feel overwhelmed and out of control.

Recently, over 1.7 million students took the SAT, while over 1.92 million took the ACT. For too many of these students, the process was intensely painful. What about you and your family? Is there more chaos than control? If you're in chaos, worrying that you're a bad test taker or avoiding any talk about test taking, you can breathe a sigh of relief. Whether using a tutor or other resource, you can improve your skills and confidence and have the energy to prepare for the ACT or SAT—and study for your courses. The information in this chapter will help make your test experience less puzzling and more positive.

How Important are College Admissions Tests Such as the ACT and SAT?

Students apply to colleges from many different high schools across the nation. How can colleges compare these students and decide which are ready for college work and, ultimately, graduation? One way of comparing students is to administer a standard test and then compare the scores. When you take the ACT or SAT, you answer the question, "How do my skills compare with those of other students in my grade across the nation?"

College admissions test scores are called "high-stakes" tests because they strongly influence your future educational options. In addition, they trigger stress and, when you don't do well, they can damage your self-confidence.

It is important to remember that, although they are an important factor, college admissions tests are but one of many factors considered by colleges and universities. Admissions committees review your application materials, trying to see you as a whole person rather than only a test score or grade point average (GPA).

Similarly, you and your family need to view your ACT or SAT test preparation in a larger perspective. It's best to think of college admissions tests not as singular event, but as a process. This process:

- Clearly shows what you know on a standardized measure. Given the competitiveness of college curricula, you need the information provided from test results to identify your strengths and weaknesses. When necessary, you can use it to decide when and how to improve in your areas of vulnerability.

- Effectively prepares you for the academic rigors of college. The material covered within each test is similar to the information and tasks that you will face once in college. For example, the writing section prepares you for completing essay questions under timed conditions in college courses.

- Actively engages you in "growing up." Those students who assume responsibility for studying and practicing for college admissions tests can develop many of the self-management skills required during the first years of college: setting a study schedule, reviewing the basics, and taking practice tests.

Therefore, it is to your advantage to be actively involved in the process of preparing for taking (and, often, retaking) the ACT and/or SAT. In addition, learning to take "high-stakes" tests is an increasingly important skill. Many other tests are required as part of, for instance, the admissions process for graduate programs or professional licensing in certain fields.

Sam, a high school freshman interested in law, says, "The testing never ends; school tests, SATs, AP tests, then tests to get into law school, tests to stay in law school, tests to get a license, and then you have to keep taking courses to keep your license. You can't escape."

Do you just hate those worrisome tests? It is important to note that there are colleges that do not require either the ACT or SAT. These colleges cater to students with special talents or interests. In such cases, you may be required to develop a portfolio or prepare for an audition, but you can bypass an admission test.

Why are the PSAT and PLAN Important?

The PSAT is a preliminary, 2-hour SAT that assesses reading, grammar, and mathematical ability. Students take the PSAT in October of their junior years of high school. Unlike with the SAT, there is no essay or writing section, scores are not sent to colleges, and, since high school juniors are typically just beginning Algebra II at test time, most of the Algebra II topics found on the SAT are not included.

After taking the PSAT, students automatically receive a copy of their test booklet, their results, and the publisher's correct answers. Questions are classified as most *easy*, *medium*, or *difficult*. Students, parents, and school personnel frequently attach little importance to the PSAT, thinking it is "only" a practice test. However, the results provide important information to you, your teachers or coaches, and your parents. Here are a few questions to ask when you review the results of the PSAT:

- What is the difference between my verbal and mathematics scores? If there is more than a 20- or 30-point difference, discuss with your parents the need for a tutor in the area that is weakest.

- At what level of difficulty are questions that I answer correctly? For example, some students are accurate with questions classified by the testmaker as "easy." These students need to learn more vocabulary or brush up on calculations so they answer correctly more questions classified as "medium" or "hard". Other students correctly answer some "easy" and some "hard" questions. These students may need to slow down and bring better focus when reading questions and noticing details. This slowing down process helps reduce silly mistakes.

- Did I finish the test? If you did not complete the test, your score may improve when you practice reading faster, doing the items that you know first, or just increasing your awareness of time during the test.

PSAT scores are also important for other reasons. In addition to preparing students for the SAT, the test also functions as the National Merit Scholarship Qualifying Test (NMSQT). Students who do well on the PSAT are entered into the competition to become National Merit Scholars. In addition, PSAT scores may be used for state-supported financial awards and a variety of special scholarships. So, while a good PSAT score will not help you get into college, it might help pay for college. For many students, this might make the PSAT just as important as the SAT. When students are in need of scholarships, they should study and prepare for the PSAT during the summer before entering the junior year of high school.

The PLAN is a 10th-grade pre-ACT assessment program designed to help students improve their planning and preparation for postsecondary education. Like the PSAT, the PLAN does not include the essay option, and scores on it are not sent to colleges. Scores on the PLAN, however, are a way to qualify for a number of scholarships. One useful feature of this examination is the career inventory, since it may be the first time you receive such information in a printed systematic format.

How Important are Advanced Placement and SAT Subject Tests?

Advanced Placement (AP) Tests and SAT Subject Tests are optional, hour-long tests in particular subject areas such as mathematics, history, or English. Some reports indicate that students who participate in AP courses have significantly better college grades and college graduation rates, and there are increasing numbers of students who are taking such courses and exams.

AP courses provide the opportunity to do college work while you are in high school. Upon completion of such a course, you register to take a national examination to demonstrate your competence in the subject. The College Board's Advanced Placement Program offers thirty-seven courses in 22 subject areas.

It is important to talk with both your school counselor and the admissions officer at the colleges you are considering attending about the necessity for taking AP courses. Also ask whether it is always necessary to take the AP exam if you have taken AP courses.

Don't assume automatic granting of college credit just because you take an AP course. Colleges have different methods of deciding how many college credits to grant in advanced placement. The decision depends not only on your score, but also on the college policies, your major, and, of course, whether you want to use them, considering all the factors involved.

You can use AP courses to:

- Earn credits toward a degree
- Place into advanced classes
- Provide an edge in the admissions process
- Provide additional academic challenge

The benefits of taking such courses include the fact that you can get college credit by signing up and paying $92 to take the test, and thus not pay regular tuition for the course when in college. With the use of advanced placement credits, some students can graduate earlier or fulfill the requirements for a double major. For example, David was a whiz at science and math. He took eleven AP courses and received 32 college credits when he entered the School of Engineering at a major research university. Money was tight, and this plan also allowed him to graduate in three years rather than four.

Here's a word of warning. An AP course may or may not adequately prepare you for the rigors of college work. Sometimes students who are exempted from an introductory level college course via advanced placement do not have the deep understanding or skill to succeed in the next course in the college sequence. It's good to remember that reduce fees are available.

Scores on the SAT Subject Tests show your achievement in specific high school subjects. Some very competitive colleges require at least three such examinations for admission. Colleges use these scores to:

- Assess your mastery in the subject
- Compare you to other students during admissions
- Help with course placement during the freshman year
- Advise you about course selection

For example, Ellie's high school was not highly ranked. Although she had a high GPA, she was afraid that colleges ranked as "very competitive" would not view her grades favorably when compared to those of others who went to more prestigious high schools. When she applied to an Eastern women's college, she took biology, writing, and American history subject tests. She was able to get funding for these tests from the College Board. Her high scores on the Subject Tests provided a more dependable measure of her academic achievement. In addition, these tests bolstered her application for a merit scholarship.

To do well on the AP or SAT Subject Tests you need to learn, remember, and apply ideas and facts from your high school courses. Too often, you do "empty" homework—you locate and write answers to homework questions rather than learn the material, and then you memorize facts before a test. For example, Marie earned a B on a test covering World War II. The next week, her coach asked her to name the Axis powers. She remembered Germany and Italy, but forgot Japan. How prepared will she be for the AP test in World History? How often do you have an experience like this student's? It's not enough to memorize facts the night before a test if you want to be adequately prepared to use the information on standardized tests or, for that matter, on finals.

Here's a learning/self-test activity called the Blank Page Exercise to help you learn on a day-by-day basis:

Without referring to your notes or book, write a few sentences to summarize the main ideas of your homework or reading assignment. Then add a few facts and examples. Refer back to your notes or book to check your accuracy and completeness.

If you spend 5 minutes in this way, you'll see what you know and don't know. Not only will you actually remember the information, but also you'll be better prepared to listen and participate in class. Your understanding and memory will soar!

AP and SAT Subject Tests are optional. Don't fall into the trap of spending too much time and energy preparing for these tests when you need to spend time studying for school tests and improving your grades. Talk to your counselor or admissions officer about the number of these courses and tests to take given your particular academic standing and the colleges of your choice. If you decide to take one or more of these courses, space them out. Try to avoid scheduling the tests during school finals.

How Should I Prepare for These Tests?

College admissions tests serve as external measures of what you have learned during your previous school years. Therefore, consider the courses you take each year as part of your ACT/SAT test preparation. For example, the more you learn the vocabulary and facts from your academic courses, the better prepared you are to deal with the content or knowledge covered on college admissions tests.

In addition to having command over the information from your academic courses, you need the test taking and the stress management skills that help you answer the SAT/ACT questions with speed, accuracy, and endurance.

- Work hard in school. Develop knowledge and skills from your courses, study for classroom tests, and earn a grade point average (GPA) that truly reflects your potential.

- Develop effective study and test-taking skills. Effective work habits help musicians, athletes, and artists to develop their talents and achieve their goals. The same idea applies to you as a student. Are you a student who waits until the last minute, stuffing knowledge into her or his head the night before the test? If so, you may earn good grades on tests and quizzes but not on final examinations. Remember, your GPA should reflect real knowledge, not merely quick memorization of facts. Scheduling time to study and self-test will help you to improve your scores on school and college admissions tests. Practice makes perfect and helps to reduce stress.

- Pay particular attention to the vocabulary included within your courses. Every textbook provides a list of words that are critical for understanding the main ideas of the course. Often, college admissions tests include these vocabulary words. If you hate reading and vocabulary lists, listen to audio recordings or watch movies of great books. Summer is a great time to upgrade or review vocabulary, math, or writing skills. Even a few sessions with a tutor or coach will help you learn higher-level vocabulary.

- Be honest when you're not doing well in your coursework. Test yourself to assess how well you are doing. For example, once a month, do some of your math homework problems without looking at your notes. Do these problems under timed conditions. How well do you remember the formulas or steps? If your grades, reading, or understanding of math, science, or social studies is lagging, then work with your classroom teacher or get a tutor. If test stress rears its ugly head during school or preliminary college admissions tests, then talk about it with parents, teachers, or counselors. Just say something like, "These tests give me the jitters, do you have any suggestions?" Often you can learn some simple strategies to help alleviate the stress and better enable you to do your best on tests.

- Begin early to familiarize yourself with ACT and SAT and use the information to plan when, how, and with whom to study. For example, in your sophomore year, begin to look at test books and review information on ACT/SAT websites. You should register to take preliminary examinations (PSAT/PLAN) to give you some idea of what it is like to take such tests and, perhaps, become eligible for scholarships.

How Do the SAT and the ACT Compare?

According to SAT and ACT websites, both tests are designed to assess students' knowledge and skills accumulated during secondary education. For example, the SAT attempts to assess student reasoning based on knowledge and skills developed by students in their school coursework. The formal name of the SAT is the SAT Reasoning Test. The redesigned SAT is closely aligned with the Core Curriculum.

The ACT appears to place greater emphasis on achievement (what you have learned) than on aptitude or reasoning (your ability to learn or think). The ACT also draws questions from content covered in the secondary school curriculum. For example, someone with little background in science, but a Master's degree in reading could not answer science questions on the ACT just based on her reading skills.

Both tests require students to work under timed conditions. The redesigned SAT requires advanced reading and vocabulary, with an emphasis on critical analysis. If you're a math whiz and hate reading, take the ACT. The ACT is accepted by all US colleges and universities.

The tests are different in several important ways:

SAT (www.collegeboard.com)

- 3 hours (plus 50 minutes for the optional Essay) there is one prompt.
- Two scores: Reading and Writing, and Mathematics (800 points for each section with a total possible score of 1600)
- Evidence-based Reading and Writing Test (52 items, 65 minutes) and Writing and Language Test (44 items, 35 minutes)
- Mathematics section includes Algebra II content: (58 items, 80 minutes)
- Greater stress on vocabulary, but little science content
- Can be taken multiple times: new rules allow the student to select which scores to report to colleges
- No penalty for guessing. Calculators are not allowed for some math questions.

ACT (www.act.org)

- 2 hours, 55 minutes
- 4 Parts: English (75 items, 45 minutes), Mathematics (60 items, 60 minutes), Reading (40 items, 35 minutes), and Science (40 items, 35 minutes) (maximum score 36 points)
- Optional 30-minute essay
- No penalty for guessing
- Mathematics section does not include Algebra II content
- More questions based on school subject matter
- Can be taken multiple times: only the scores from the selected test day are reported to colleges

In 2015, the average ACT score was 21.0 out of a possible 36 points. In 2015, the Average SAT score was 1490 out of a possible 2400. The new SAT, administered in 2016, will have a possible score of 1600.

Which Tests Should I Schedule and When?

One key question facing college-bound students is, "Should I take the ACT or SAT or both?" In a nutshell, find the test on which you score highest, and stick with that test. The ACT is better for those with shorter attention spans, lower energy, or poor writing skills. The SAT is better for highly verbal students with strong analytical skills. One great way to pick the test you're stronger on is to take both the PLAN (Preliminary ACT) and the PSAT and see which you score best on.

Since colleges in the United States usually try to attract a geographically diverse student body, virtually all of them accept either SAT or ACT scores. Check the requirements of the top schools in which you are interested. If schools of your choice accept both the ACT and the SAT, then you can decide which test to take based on your particular interests and skills. If you are unsure about which test to take, then take a practice or diagnostic test for each one. Practice materials are available from your school counselor, commercial practice books, or websites such as www.collegeboard.com or www.act.org. See how you feel taking each test and how you score. Review the results with your counselor, teacher, tutor, or coach to decide on which test you can best show what you know.

The prevailing wisdom is that ACT is more closely linked to the school curriculum. If you do well in your high school courses, then take the ACT. The ACT is a best choice for students who do well in science. It is also best for students who have less developed vocabulary and reading skills. Students who become tired, bored or frustrated easily may want to avoid the SAT since it demands high focus and concentration on all sections. In addition, it includes analysis of data in charts and graphs.

Some states, like Michigan, use the SAT as their state assessment. In such cases, the essay is mandatory and therefore, the test is almost an hour longer than the ACT. The redesigned SAT appears more tedious and complex. If you must take it as a state assessment, but don't score well, practice and take the ACT and send only those scores to the colleges of your choice.

You can take the ACT or SAT as many times as you want. Many students take the tests twice, first as a junior and again as a senior. Twice is usually enough, unless you are going to take more time to prepare, take a special course, work with a new tutor or coach, or were ill or "stressed to the max" when you took it previously. If you take the ACT or SAT in the spring of your junior year, you can schedule the necessary study, remedial, and test prep activities for the following summer or early fall.

Use these tips after you receive the results of your ACT or SAT tests:

- Write to the publisher to request a copy of your test.

- Review each section and identify the types of questions that you answered correctly and incorrectly.

- Discuss the results with your teacher, tutor, or counselor.

- List your strengths and weaknesses.

- Decide methods to help you increase your test-taking or academic skills. For example, learn the 10 most common grammatical rules or mistakes so that you pick up more points on the multiple-choice questions and on the writing section of the SAT.

Only retake these tests if you have done something specific to help you improve your score. If you haven't studied, used a tutor, or practiced answering test questions, your score will probably not change very much.

When Do I Prepare For High-Stakes Tests?

When you learn how to manage your time and your tasks, you learn how to manage your academic and social life. With respect to the ACT/SAT, you benefit by scheduling activities on a yearly, quarterly, weekly, and daily basis. You might say, "I'm busy and don't care too much about these tests. What difference will it make? I'm only in 9th grade."

If you want high performance, then planning and scheduling are important. Can you imagine an Olympic athlete who doesn't have a long-term plan? Think of the time between 9th and 12th grades as a journey from middle school to college. Each year you are in a different place, doing different activities, but all the while you're moving toward your college destination. There are some activities that you can schedule with the help of a parent, coach, or counselor. Just completing a few activities each year prevents you from feeling overwhelmed, underprepared, and out of control. Planning helps you to improve your test performance and reduces stress. Use a multi-year schedule to guide your ACT/SAT preparation activities.

What Can I Do to Improve My Scores?

Find out your scores on the PSAT, PLAN, ACT, SAT, AP, or SAT Subject Tests, and decide whether your score reflects your real abilities and skills. If you feel you can do better, then think about what it takes to earn a better score. Although you may do well on your school tests, when taking a test in school you're not taking a 2- or 3-hour test or competing against students across the nation.

Take a look at the average scores from recent graduating classes to see how competitive you are.

New SAT: There are 800 possible points for each of two sections, with a total possible score of 800 points.

ACT: Out of 36 possible points on the ACT, the average score nationally for a recent graduating class was 21.1.

Here are some strategies to help you improve your scores:
Scoring high on the SAT and ACT requires that you experience peak performance, including answering questions on demand, with speed and accuracy, for over three hours, under distracting and stressful conditions. There is research that indicates that coaching and practice has the potential of raising SAT scores. For example, in one study, scores on the math section of the SAT improved by 20–30 points (see http://www.fairtest.org/examarts/Spring%2002/SAT%/20Coaching.html).

Most athletes' performance improves when they have the services of a coach. Coaches observe athletes' performances and give them pointers about the competition and how to best use their strengths. The same is true for students who face ACT/SAT challenges. Coaching provides information and feedback about what to learn, how to learn it, and how best to apply your knowledge and skills during the test. Whether teacher, tutor or coach, make sure that the person helping you:

- works with high school students
- understands the nature and challenges of the ACT or SAT

• explains how you can improve when you do practice questions

You have choices. Here are some methods you can consider:

• Commercial test preparations courses are good for students who enjoy a group situation, interchange during practice sessions, and the motivation provided by the instructor. Such courses, however, are very expensive. Don't take a course unless you want to take it and are committed to getting something out of it. For example, although Teresa didn't care about taking a course, her parents registered her for a once-weekly 6–9 p.m. SAT course. She arrived hungry and tired after field hockey practice. As the instructor droned on, she doodled and dozed. Her parents spent the money and she wasted her time. Also, attendance alone doesn't guarantee results. If you sign up for a commercial course, attend at a time of day when you are alert, attend all the sessions, do the practice work, and ask for special help if you need it. These courses include up to 35 hours and provide practice in both reading and math.

• Tutoring or coaching is the best option for students who are unmotivated, distractible, anxious, or lacking skills in one particular area such as reading, writing, or math. The tutor, teacher, or coach, can review the types of question or skill that are most challenging, provide special explanations and strategies, and help the student stay on track. For some students, working one-on-one makes the test prep process less arduous and tedious. Consider making an audio recording of your tutoring sessions. Replaying a session helps you remember strategies and practice on your own. It may take 3 to 6 months to improve your skills.

Work with a tutor that you like and find useful; nice is not enough. There are tutors who are retired teachers, college students, or current teachers who tutor on the weekends. Ask at your school for a list of available tutors or other resources. Here are some questions that your parents can ask when looking for a tutor:

— *What is your educational background?*

— *How long have you been helping students with the ACT/SAT?*

— *What subject matter is your specialty? (For example, some tutors have gotten high scores on the ACT/SATs but don't have any teaching experience. Some tutors are great for reading, but horrible for math.)*

— *Do you have any references? Is it possible to speak to previous clients or their parents?*

• Self-study is a less expensive but a very useful test prep method, if you have previously demonstrated your ability to work on your own. For example, if you have a study schedule and follow it, then you have the basic study habits that are needed to add ACT/SAT study to your schedule. There are a variety of resources to help you understand the test formats, directions, questions types, and patterns of the tests. These include:

— *Practice books with diagnostic tests, many with accompanying interactive software.*

— *Software that delivers test questions and answers to a cell phone screen. You can order questions that are easy, medium, or difficult and get immediate feedback about each answer including explanations about why it is correct or incorrect.*

— *Cartoon books with SAT vocabulary or crossword puzzles.*

— *Classic books such as Wuthering Heights and Frankenstein with SAT vocabulary words and definitions in boldface.*

Whether in a commercial class, with a tutor or coach, or on your own, you need to practice answering questions. The questions on admissions tests are different and more difficult than those you confront in school. For example, the SAT math section includes questions that involve mathematical models of real-life situations. According to www.collegeboard.com, "a question might present information about the projected sales of a product at various prices and ask for a mathematical model in the form of a graph or equation that represents product sales as a function of price." Wow. That's not your average school test question.

When Should I Deal with Test-taking or School Problems?

Keep in mind the phrase, "There's no time like the present." Part of your everyday education is to learn the facts and vocabulary in your courses, upgrade your reading writing and math skills, and polish your test-taking skills.

Additionally, there are some factors to consider if you want to make good decisions about scheduling test prep activities. Use the chart below to think about any special needs or gaps that need attention. You need to prepare differently if you fail geometry and need to upgrade your math skills than if you forget facts and details after you study.

For example, Bill feels smart, but doesn't do well on tests. His memory fails him when it comes to reading comprehension and test taking. In the spring of his 10th grade, his parents speak to his teachers about providing memory techniques in his various courses. In addition, he goes to a library-sponsored summer program to improve his reading skills.

The yearly "If/Then" chart below provides some suggestions about what and when to plan based on different circumstances:

	IF:	THEN during the School Year:	THEN during the Summer:
9th Grade	You didn't have to study very much in middle school...	Understand that you need to spend more time on homework and learning. Begin high school with the idea that each course counts.	Take a writing or reading improvement course, or explore a special interest experience on a college campus.
10th Grade	You received a C- in math or your grades do not reflect the amount of time you study...	Work with your math teacher or other tutor or consider talking to a school counselor, social worker, psychologist about your difficulties.	Get a tutor to review coursework or have your parent call an expert to investigate the possibility of hidden learning problems.
11th Grade	You earned a significantly lower score in reading than in math on the PSAT...	Work after school with a reading teacher or study the verbal section with a friend once a week.	Work one-on-one with an ACT/SAT coach, take a commercial course, or do practice exercises on your own or with a friend using practice books and software.
12th Grade	Test stress interferes with test scores...	Take yoga, do more exercise, and learn stress management techniques such as deep breathing.	Exercise, rest and relax. Take a stress management course at the local hospital or college.

What Reading Strategies Are Helpful?

Every ACT/SAT practice book has a section explaining and illustrating how to improve you score on the reading section. The advice is to try to understand what you are reading and learn how to read between the lines. It is not enough to look for facts and details; you need to look for key ideas and then find deeper meaning and relationships within or between passages. You may not have to do this type of reading in school, so you may need special practice for the ACT or SAT. Try to review the instructions about effective reading with a friend, or with a tutor, teacher, or coach.

Learn the instructions for this and all sections before you take the test. When you realize that you need to find the best answer, not just any answer, you become more willing to read every choice, rather than jump at the first choice that is possible. So why waste your valuable time reading directions when you can spend the time checking your answers? Learn the directions prior to the test so you can save time and build confidence.

Types of Reading

The reading passages gauge your reading skills using selections from popular literature, history, or science. On the SAT Evidence-Based Reading and Writing section, you read passages of 800 words and answer 10 questions or compare 2 shorter passages and answer questions. You will read passages with informational graphics such as tables, graphs, and charts. On the SAT Writing and Language test, you'll be the editor and need to use rules of grammar, punctuation , words in context, and style.

Do practice exercises! You will notice that different types of questions require different types of reading skills. Once you understand the design of the test questions, you can answer with greater speed and accuracy.

For example, the Critical Reading Section of the ACT includes passages of prose fiction, social studies, and science. After reading a social studies passage, you'll need to answer questions that refer to key names, definitions and facts, causes and effects, and chronology. When reading prose fiction, you are not reading to enjoy the story, but to analyze the plot, character development, and relationships between characters. With such reading, you need to read at a deeper level than just identification of facts. You need to draw inferences and observe similarities.

Realize that to excel on the ACT or SAT you may need to use different reading skills in the reading versus the math sections. For example, Barbara is an avid and skilled reader, scoring in the 99th percentile on the Critical Reading Section of the SAT. She assumes that she can read the math questions at the same pace at which she reads the reading passages. However, she is less skilled in math than in reading, and she misses important details. This contributes to a high error rate, even when she understands the operations. She improves her score by slowing her reading rate to ensure that she understands the questions, notes the details, and more fully works out her answers on the test booklet.

Identify and learn words that are included within the reading passage and questions. Say any unfamiliar words aloud. For example, in a review of his PSAT results, Josh's coach identifies a few mistakes in the sentence completion section categorized as easy. Josh looks at a word and says, "I've never heard of this word." His coach says, "Say it out loud." Josh says, "aRID." The coach responds, "If a word doesn't sound familiar, then say the word again but place the accent on a different syllable. "Arid," says Josh. "Yeah, like in the commercial for Arid Extra Dry?" How many extra points can Josh gain if he pauses to think about a word or meaning?

Six Steps to Help You Improve Your Reading Comprehension While Doing Practice Exercises:

1) Read the introduction of the passage and say or write the main idea. This arouses your curiosity and helps focus your attention.

2) Review the questions to see how many deal with main ideas, facts or details, inferences, or vocabulary. For example, if you like facts and figures, and, if you notice that many questions about a particular passage include phrases such as "infer that…," "the tone is…," or "implies that…," then you might want to skip that passage until you have completed other passages that include more factual questions. When you review the questions first, you can decide the order in which you will read the passages. Feeling that you have a choice reduces your stress and increases your focus.

3) Read the first line of each paragraph to identify the way the information is organized. For example, identify if the passage provides comparisons, identifies causes and effects, or traces a sequence of events.

4) Answer any questions to which the answers become immediately apparent.

5) While reading a passage, watch for signal words, such as "in conclusion" or "in contrast." Say the message in your own words, summarize the main idea, and visualize the ideas as you read. These activities help you to comprehend the information as you read it.

6) As you answer a question, underline the location in the passage that provides the answer. This helps you see small differences and avoid mistakes.

What Writing Strategies Are Helpful?

"I feel a sense of doom when I think of writing an essay under timed pressure." Stephen is voicing the feeling of many students. Whether taking the SAT or the ACT, you need to know how to plan, organize and write legibly. You need to be able to state your opinion and defend a position. The ACT writing section is optional and requires you to write an essay in which you take a side of an issue and defend it. The SAT writing section is optional, requiring analytical skills to read a passage and analyze the author's argument.

Recently about 30% of those taking the ACT took the writing section, with an average score of 7.7 on a scale ranging from 2 to 12.

If you hate writing or feel anxious about it, you have some options. One option is to avoid the writing requirement by registering to take only the ACT. Another option is to take the SAT and apply to colleges that place little value on or ignore the writing score for admissions purposes.

On both tests, you have 25 minutes to read the essay question and answer it. You read a quotation and a question asking you to support a position with examples and to use your reading, observations, or experiences. Unlike math, with which you can use an aid such as a calculator, there is no typing or spell check. On the Essay the section of the SAT, you have 50 minutes to read a prompt and analyze an argument. You read a passage of 650-750 words You need to use your reasoning and the textual evidence from the reading. Your task is to analyze an author's argument and explain how the author persuades an audience. This is a complex and difficult task, especially within a 50-minute time period.

As an academic coach, I advise students to learn how to write under such conditions; the skills needed to do so will also be needed later for answering essay questions in college. Here are some tips to help you in crashing through barriers to writing:

- Become an expert in a few typical topics, such as loyalty, leadership, or friendship.

- Be on the lookout for controversial topics presented in newspapers, talk shows, or magazines.

- Review topics and sample essays provided online or in practice books.

- Practice writing, first without time limits and then with time limits.

- Take 5 minutes to plan and organize your thoughts before you begin writing. Think before you write, and read the entire question before you plan.

- Spend time with a tutor reviewing grammatical rules, since there are portions of these tests designed to assess grammatical skills.

- Avoid sarcasm and humor, since it is difficult to do it well in writing, especially under timed conditions.

- Use your own vocabulary.

- Improve legibility. If your handwriting is messy, take a handwriting course or get the services of an occupational therapist.

- Distinguish fact from opinion.

- Select a side and defend it.

How Are Charts and Diagrams Helpful?

There is a saying, "One picture is worth a thousand words." There is great truth in this saying when it comes to studying for and taking the ACT or SAT. You can use a visual aid such as a chart, sketch, or diagram when you answer questions in the reading, math, or writing sections. For example, in the writing section of the SAT, you have to write in an organized way about a topic. You may feel that the topic is irrelevant. You may be tense, tired, or irritated. You may lack the motivation to put in the thinking effort required to develop a decent piece of writing.

Diagrams to the rescue! The use of a diagram helps you focus on the main ideas to develop and organize your thoughts, and to enhance your efficiency. Several basic types of diagrams are particularly helpful. For example, for topics requiring you to sequence or trace events, use a timeline. For topics that require comparison and contrast or a pro/con argument, use a simple T diagram. Use these and other graphic organizers when practicing for the writing section of the SAT, developing school papers, or composing your personal statement for college applications.

Question:
Should 18-year-olds be allowed to vote?

Question:
How did I develop my passion for music?

Question:
What were the causes of World War II?

PRO | CON

TIMELINE

CAUSES   EFFECTS

How Do I Manage Time During Tests?

The time allotments allowed for high school test taking may be ample or even lenient. Even during final examinations, you may not experience problems managing your time. In contrast, the time limits imposed by the ACT/SAT are strictly enforced and create new stress for many students. Here are some time management tips to use while you are taking the ACT or SAT:

- Don't be overwhelmed by the length of the test. No section is more than 30 minutes, so think of completing each section rather than taking a long, multi-hour test.

- Don't get bummed if one section is especially difficult. Take time to give yourself a pep talk, take a few deep breaths, and move on.

- Pace yourself and don't spend too much time on any one question. Do the easiest questions first, since all questions are of equal value.

- Take time to check accuracy.

- Take time to write notes or work out problems. This helps you notice details and avoid "silly" mistakes.

How Do I Manage Test Stress?

Do you "freak out" at the mention of the ACT or SAT? Many students do—and why not?

The ACT or SAT presents a new, unique, and daunting challenge. You have to take a high stakes test that is 3-hours long, and you must answer questions that are generally different from, and more difficult than, those on typical school tests. To add even more pressure, some students feel overwhelmed when they must work under timed conditions, knowing that they have gaps in reading or math skills, or have a long history of negative experiences with tests.

Some stress helps you become alert and more focused. Too much stress, however, slows you down and reduces your attention, motivation, and accuracy.

How does test stress affect you? Stress may sneak up and trigger symptoms without you realizing that it is rearing its ugly head. Become aware of the physical and emotional signs of test stress. Review a list of possible symptoms and check any that apply to you.

Physical Symptoms

- Headaches
- Muscle tension/neck or backaches
- Rapid heartbeat
- Fast, shallow breathing
- Stomach upset
- Sleep disturbances
- Sweating palms

Psychological Symptoms

- Distractibility
- Short attention span
- Poor memory
- Poor organization
- Irritability
- Mood swings
- Fatigue

If you have more than a few of these symptoms—occasional instances of emotional or physical stress—then talk about it to some trusted adult, such as your parent or other family member, physician, or counselor.

Let's get more specific about the effect that stress can have on you during test time.

Think about the SAT or ACT while you read the following statements. Check any that apply to you.

____ 1. I freeze when I get to a question I can't do.

____ 2. I feel pressured when I take timed tests.

____ 3. I make negative statements such as "I'll never be able to get a good score."

___ 4. I have interfering thoughts (worries) while I'm taking the test.

___ 5. I get headaches or other physical symptoms of stress.

If you checked even one statement, you can benefit from using a few simple stress management strategies.

Of course, there are helpful and non-helpful ways of dealing with stress. For example, avoidance is a common, but non-helpful, method of responding to stress. The best stress management strategy is the avoidance of avoidance. A study plan is a great way of reducing stress since it gives you a path to action and a better sense of control.

So, what can you do to combat the jitters on ACT or SAT test day? Here are some tried and true tips:

- Before you get to the test:

    — *Check that you have necessary materials. For example, bring pencils, snacks, and extra batteries for you calculator.*

    — *Arrive early to avoid feeling rushed.*

    — *Avoid unnecessary anxiety-related pre-exam talk.*

    — *Think positive thoughts, such as "I studied and will do well."*

    — *Create positive images. Before the test, picture yourself working productively.*

    — *Rehearse. Before the actual test date, take a full-length practice test under actual test conditions. For example, go to a library and take the test.*

- When you arrive at the testing site:

    — *Use a warm-up routine. For example, stretch and take deep breaths.*

    — *Read directions out loud.*

    — *Write helpful hints to yourself such as "Take your time," or "Take one-minute breaks."*

    — *Visualize a time when you successfully practiced some test questions.*

    — *Tense and relax muscles between test sections. Chew gum.*

    — *Know what and when to skip.*

    — *Use breaks to stretch and have a healthy, high-energy snack.*

Some students experience stress far ahead of the actual ACT/SAT test date. Even before they pick up the practice book, they get butterflies, see themselves failing, or feel irritable. Here are some simple stress management strategies to use before you begin to study at home or in the library. Review the list of possible stress busters and check any that are of interest to you. If you do not see any items of interest, then make a list of your own ideas, or brainstorm with a friend or relative.

- Use a journal to describe your feelings.

- Stop drinking/eating caffeine-laden items.
- Sit in a rocker or take a bubble bath or warm shower.
- Spray energizing scents such as evergreen.
- Find something humorous to read, watch, or listen to.
- Play an entertaining or amusing game for a few minutes. Use a puzzle, yoyo, or Slinky.

If you have persistent symptoms, talk to your parent and consider discussing the situation with your family physician.

How Do I Develop an Action Plan?

It takes more than good intentions to do well on a college admissions test. It takes time, organization, and hard work. In other words, you need to move from talk to action.

A test-prep plan provides the means for converting good intentions into meaningful test preparation. Good preparation results in good scores, but great preparation leads to the best scores possible for you. There is no one best test-prep plan. Review the following eight components and develop your own test-prep strategy:

1) What do I want?

Set a Goal: Although your short-term goal may be an improved score, your long-term goal is to show what you know when performing under very competitive conditions. Your goal is to feel that your study leads to you to feeling greater control, competence, and confidence. Test taking is a life-long skill. Learning to do well on tests such as the ACT or SAT helps to prepare you for the challenge of taking college-level multiple choice and essay tests. It is risky to set a goal to achieve an ACT score that is hundreds of points higher than a previous score. Discuss with your counselor or tutor a range of realistically possible scores. Is your desired score a dream or a real possibility?

2) What do I need to do?

Identify Responsibilities for You and Your Parent: Since you are the one who is taking the ACT and/or SAT, you will do best if you assume responsibility for the studying. List activities for which you will be responsible. Identify how your parents (or tutor/coach) will help you to implement your plan and improve your skills. This removes many sources of conflict and allows you to focus your effort on studying rather than bickering.

3) Where Will I Study Best?

Identify Effective Study Conditions: It is important for you to become aware of the ways in which your surroundings help or hinder your study efforts. Your plan should specify where and with whom you want to study or do practice questions. Will you work with a friend? Do you need a tutor? For many students, the idea of an "electonic lockdown" provides the quiet think time needed to learn and review material for the ACT or SAT. This means that for 20-minute periods, you shut off the television, iPod, cell phone, and computer. Seriously reduce the distractions from these technological wonders. If you are an unbeliever, do an experiment. Try doing some problems with loud music and some without. Most often, your speed and accuracy will improve when you remove distractions.

4) When and for How Long Will I Study?

Set a Schedule: You have a busy life. Unless you schedule study times, little study occurs. Use a regular calendar that covers the time between the current date and the date of the ACT or SAT. Schedule weekly study sessions for you (and possibly a friend) and for a course or tutor. Registering for a course doesn't take the place of studying and, for example, learning new vocabulary words.

5) How Should I Study?

Identify Strategies: Read the introductory information in the practice books, talk to your teachers, ask your friends, or hire a tutor. You need to know test-taking strategies that help you do your best on the ACT or SAT. For example, the reading sections of these tests require skills that you do not practice in your high school classes. You need someone to show you how best to read and answer the questions.

6) Who Can Help?

Find Resources: Find out about the resources available in your community. For example, some schools and libraries offer free services. Some tutoring services offer packages for college admissions test preparation that are less expensive than the standard commercial courses. Investigate online programs, since they may be cheaper and possibly shared by several students. For example, the Kahn Academy has free, personlized SAT study resources for all students at https://KahnAcademy.org/SAT.

7) Who Can I Study With?

Find a Study Buddy: You may be a student who benefits from working with a friend or with a small group. You can take a practice test in one or more areas, such as math or reading. Compare answers and discuss how different students arrived at various answers. Work for 15 to 20 minutes, take a short break, and then resume. You and your friends can act as your own coaches. You practice, review how you did, and identify how you can do better. Have fun together while you're learning.

8) How Much Will it Cost?

Set a Budget: Costs are an important consideration. Talk about them with your parents. Discuss the estimated costs of various alternatives. Sometimes it is cheaper to hire a college student as a tutor than to register for a commercial course. How many practice books clutter your friends' closets, half used—or for that matter, never opened? Ask your friends if they know of others who have practice books that you can use.

Here is a sample of a handy form that Dylan used to prepare for his college admissions test:

Date: Summer	Name: Dylan
Goals	1. Increase the number of correct math or reading questions answered during each tutoring session. 2. Practice using effective reading strategies so that I can complete the test. 3. Learn 20 unfamiliar words found within the Sentence Completion Section of the SAT. 4. Fine-tune the grammar and writing skills.
Responsibilities	• Mom goes with me to buy the book and pays for the tutor. • I pay attention to the tutor and do the practice exercises. UGH!
Study Conditions	• Go to the library twice a week and work with Tony for 40 minutes. We do 20 minutes of math questions and then talk about the answers. • Try the "electronic lockdown" for 20 minutes when I need to memorize theorems.
Schedule	• Tuesdays from 4:30 to 5:30 p.m. with the reading tutor. • Work on vocabulary for no more than 20 minutes before the tutor comes.
Strategies	• After I memorize a word or theorem, write it from memory on a whiteboard, and then check it with the book. • Remember to stretch and take deep breaths between sections.
Resources	• Ask my friends which books or programs they liked best. • Talk to the tutor and decide if he is right for me.
Study Buddy	• Tony.
Budget	• See if studying alone, with Tony, and with the tutor is enough. • Consider a course in the summer if I don't do well the first time.

Use the form below to begin your ACT or SAT test preparation plan:

Date:	Name:
Goals	
Responsibilities	
Study Conditions	
Schedule	
Strategies	
Resources	
Study Buddy	
Budget	

How Can I Guarantee Disappointing Results?

If you are new to the high-stakes testing game, then you might not be aware of the foolish behaviors that can guarantee a poor performance. Fellow students who learned the hard way report that there are a number of ways to ensure that your ACT or SAT test experience yields disappointing results. *Here are a few:*

- Don't study.

- Stay up late the night before the test.

- Stuff yourself by eating unhealthy foods or highly spiced snacks the night before the test.

- Don't eat a healthy breakfast the day of the test.

- Do drink highly caffeinated drinks and get antsy or jumpy.

- Get up late and rush out of the house, perhaps forgetting your calculator.

- Tell yourself that you didn't study enough and don't deserve to get a good score.

- Resist any advice of parents, teachers, and counselors.

If, for whatever reason, your scores are lower than you want or expect, you have options and choices. Don't just say, "I'll never do well." Understand that you can take action and earn additional points. For example:

- If you understand the test and study for it. Say, "It's longer and harder than other tests, but it is still a test that I can study for and do better on next time."

- If you anticipate that your scores will be exceptionally low due to an illness or an upsetting event, you have the right to cancel the score a few days after you took the test and reschedule another test date.

- If you want to retake a test, you have the right to request your test and answer sheet. This is particularly helpful in work with a tutor or coach for identifying the types of questions you need to practice the most.

- If you suspect there was an error in scoring your test because your score does not reflect your skill levels, you can request hand scoring. It costs fifty dollars, but, in some cases, it is well worth it. Scoring mistakes do happen and have been reported by the media.

When ACT/SAT scores are low, some leeway may be given if parents are not college graduates, if a student is a member of a minority group, if a disability hinders performing well on standardized tests, or if the student possesses an extracurricular talent in an area such as music, art, or athletics. Some students identify these conditions and discuss them in their college admission essays.

If your test results are disappointing, you can retake the test. Currently, if you take a test multiple times, all of your scores are sent to the colleges you list. As of 2010, however, you will be allowed by the College Board, publisher of the SAT, to select which SAT or SAT Subject Test scores to send to colleges.

What Role(s) Can My Parents Play?

Many teens find that having their parents involved in ACT/SAT prep is a "near death" experience. This is true even when parents are nice and don't nag. As a coach, I've observed some teens "blow up" at the mere mention of the ACT or SAT by a parent. You may feel that parents have no role to play, but nothing can be further from the truth. At the very least, parents pay for registration fees or courses or tutors. If parents are willing to help, then your least responsibility is to thank them and perhaps describe one or two ways in which they can be of most assistance.

Mitch says, "My parents just don't understand how difficult some of the test questions are. They say stuff like, 'What's the big deal? We all had to take tests.'" In frustration, he blurts out, "If you think it's so easy, why don't you try a few of the math or reading questions?" His parents do try some of the questions and are amazed about how difficult and different the questions are in comparison with Mitch's typical homework. Their attitude changes and, with more empathy and support, Mitch has less stress and more motivation to prepare for the tests.

Most parents are delighted when their children assume responsibility and talk to them about what they can do to help.

You and your parents have choices. You can choose one or any combination of roles from the following list:

- **Buyer:** This is a supportive and timesaving role. Your parent provides the money and you buy the books or resources you need. Alternatively, your parent is asked to research courses, get the schedules and prices, and, after discussing options, perhaps register you for the instruction you want/need.

- **Tutor/Teacher/Coach:** This is a challenging role. Some parents are teachers and have the knowledge you need. If your relationship allows, you parent can help you learn or practice in one or more subjects. For some students, the best arrangement is to work with another family. Your parent teaches your friend and your friend's parent helps you. In any case, schedule a few sessions and then evaluate their usefulness. If you think the tutoring is useful, schedule additional sessions.

- **Advocate/Manager:** This role is required when students have a special need or disability. For example, when students have learning or attention-related disabilities, they may be eligible for test accommodations. In such cases, parents needs to talk to counselors, send in reports, and keep track of deadlines.

- **Organizer:** This role is helpful for the disorganized or somewhat disinterested student. The student asks the parent to help with tasks such as setting a schedule to study (e.g., twice a week for 35 minutes). The parent acts as the student's assistant— but doesn't nag.

- **Motivator:** This role is helpful when the ACT/SAT study task seems irrelevant or overwhelming. Your parents, grandparents, or other family members may be able to see the advantages of studying and help you to be more motivated. For example, they might suggest early college visits, a talk with a college counselor to identify schools to which you are suited, or discuss your strengths and interests. Your parents or other family members may relate the questions and concerns they had when they were growing up. One grandmother said, "You're the first girl in the family to go to college. It's tough to take these tests, but fight like a beast in the jungle. You'll see. You'll do great." With a champion like that, isn't it easier to muster the energy and find the time to do the studying required to prepare for the ACT or SAT?

Take some time to think about the ways in which your parents have been helpful in the past, and list one or two ways they might be helpful during your preparation for the ACT or SAT. Ask them how they would like to be involved. Enlist the help of other family members or friends, perhaps creating a team of support. Five to ten minutes of productive conversation about roles can reduce stress and help you to get the scores you'd like on college admissions tests.

What Are Specific Tips for Students with AD/HD and/or Learning Disabilities?

Students with disabilities are confronted by special challenges when studying for or taking the ACT or SAT. For instance, a student with a learning disability may have great difficulty keeping the marks on the answer sheet in the correct order. Some students hesitate to request accommodations. One student made the following comment: "Even though I really need more time and a quiet room, I hate the idea of accommodations. I really don't want the other kids to know about my learning disability. Also, I worry about what the college admissions counselor will think if I use the accommodations."

This student need not worry. If you take a college admissions test with an accommodation such as extended time, the publishers of the ACT and SAT no longer flag scores to indicate that the test was taken under non-standard conditions.

If you have a disability, here are a few tips:

- Start early by reviewing diagnostic reports, getting tutors, and making a plan. For example, perhaps a diagnostic report recommends that you have an accommodation such as extended time, but you have never needed it for school tests. Given the length and time pressure of college admissions tests, many counselors and coaches advise students to apply for such accommodations, even for the PSAT or PLAN.

- Understand that you must apply for accommodations to take these tests under extended time conditions. The application includes the diagnosis, the credentials of the professional who provides the diagnosis, and documentation by your school if test accommodations are used there.

- Apply early for accommodations if you need them. Your counselor needs to help with the application for accommodations. It may take months to get the accommodation.

- Remember to take your medication on the day of the test.

- Discuss with a counselor or professional how to describe your strengths, vulnerabilities, and special interests or talents in your personal statement. Remember that college admissions tests are only one part of the application process. Ask if there is any flexibility in admission criteria for students with disabilities, especially if they have other talents or special interests.

- Consider applying to colleges that have ample resources and strong support services for students with disabilities. For instance, some schools allow students with disabilities to take a lighter course load and still be considered full-time and eligible for financial aid.

What Are 10 Tips for Preparing for Those Nerve-Wracking College Admissions Tests?

1) High stakes tests are an unpleasant fact; understand the requirements of each test by reading the introductory information in a practice book.

2) Practice for the PSAT and PLAN and inquire about the use of the PSAT scores for qualifying for Merit Scholarships.

3) View your study for the ACT and SAT as an opportunity to demonstrate peak academic performance based on the knowledge and skills developed in your high school courses.

4) Develop a study plan that includes schedules, routines, and resources.

5) Gain confidence through competence; get tutors, work with teachers, practice, and review. Build your skills in areas of vulnerability or in areas not taught or practiced in your school.

6) Schedule frequent short practice sessions two or three times a week, over two or three months. Monitor your progress every other week.

7) Practice answering questions without time constraints.

8) Take at least one full-length test under timed and simulated conditions.

9) Identify and use breathing, stretching, or other stress management techniques

10) Identify small rewards for yourself as recognition of your study effort and progress.

Conclusion

"When the Going Gets Tough, the Tough Get Going." Many attribute these words to Knute Rockne, the American Football player and coach. This famous coach used this phrase to motivate peak performances of his team. This message is equally relevant to students facing the competition and pressure triggered by high-stakes college admissions tests.

The high school going gets tough at ACT/SAT time. Get tough with yourself. Imagine yourself as a fine competitor, work hard at your studies, and practice, and you will score your best on those nerve-wracking college admission tests.

Test Preparation Schedule

Freshman Year:

- Review graduation and college admission requirements with your counselor and parents. Talk to other students and family members and counselors to get an idea of which college you'd like to attend and to get an idea of the requirements for admission.

- Talk with your school counselor and your colleges of interest about the need and availability of scholarships, especially those based on scores from college admissions tests.

- Build your vocabulary and math skills by doing crossword puzzles, math games, or word problems.

Sophomore Year:

- Label folders and designate a file drawer or milk crate for college admissions test materials, including the PSAT and PLAN.

- Practice your thinking skills by playing logic games (e.g., Whiff and Poof, chess, cards, crossword puzzles, Scrabble, or Sudoku).

- Take a speech course so you will feel comfortable and competent when you interview for volunteer experiences, jobs, or college.

Junior Year:

- Talk to your teachers or other school personnel about your test-taking skills. Ask them for their advice about improving your grades.

- Take a practice PSAT. This test is over 2-hours long and it is important to know how to pace your test taking.

- Don't let exam panic set in. Make a study plan, get a tutor, and study with your friends.

- Send for college booklets and brochures to discover the range of ACT/SAT scores achieved by students who are accepted.

- Get a separate email address for correspondence about college admission tests and other college correspondence.

- In the spring, take the SAT and ACT. Based on the results, decide whether you need to improve, and if so make a plan for how to do so.

- Take summer school courses if you need to improve your skills and grades.

Senior Year:

- Register to retake the ACT or SAT to earn a higher score.

- Decide whether you will take the AP or SAT subject tests.

- Adapt the attitude that senior courses count in terms of the information and skills you need to do well in college.

- If your scores in one area of a college admissions tests is low, consider brushing up your math, verbal, or writing skills in the summer.

References & Resources

Section 1: Finding the College That Fits

Antonoff, S. R. & Friedmann, M. A. (2006) College Match, 9th Edition, Alexandria, VA: Octameron Books.

Asher, D. (2000) Cool Colleges for the Hyper-Intelligent, Self Directed, Late Blooming, and Just Plain Different, Toronto, CA: Ten Speed Press.

Fiske, E. B. (2009) The Fiske Guide to Colleges, Naperville, IL: Sourcebooks.

Fiske, E. B. & Hammond, B. G. (2001) Getting into the Right College, 2nd Edition, Naperville, IL: Sourcebooks.

Franek, R. et al. (2003) The Best Midwestern Colleges: 150 Great Schools to Consider, New York, NY: Princeton Review, Random House.

Kravets, M. B. & Wax, I. F. (2008) The K&W Guide to Colleges for Students with Learning Disabilities or Attention Deficit Disorder, New York, NY: Princeton Review, Random House.

Mathews, J. (2003) Harvard Schmarvard: Getting Beyond the Ivy League to the College That's Best For You, New York, NY: Prima Publishing, Random House.

Pope, L. (2007) Colleges That Change Lives: 40 Schools You Should Know About Even if You're Not a Straight-A-Student, New York, NY: Penguin Books.

Pope, L. (2006) Looking Beyond the Ivy League: Finding the College That's Right for You, New York, NY: Penguin Books.

Re, J. M. (2005) Financial Aid Financer: Expert Answers to College Financing Questions, 17th Edition, Alexandria, VA: Octamaron Books.

Ripple, G. G. (2001) Campus Pursuit: Making the Most of Your Visit and Interview, 9th Edition, Alexandria, VA: Octamaron Books.

___The Best 373 Colleges (2011) New York, NY: The Princeton Review, Inc.

___ Complete Book of Colleges: The Mega-Guide to 1,578 Colleges and Universities. (2011) New York, NY: The Princeton Review, Inc.

Staff at the Yale Daily News (2011) The Insider's Guide to the Colleges: Students on Campus Tell you What you Really Want to Know. New York NY: St. Martin's Griffin.

Rubenstone, S. & Dalby, S. (2002) College Admissions: A Crash Course for Panicked Parents, 3rd Edition, Lawrenceville, NY: ARCO Books, Peterson's–Thomson.

Rugg, F. E. (2009) Rugg's Recommendations on the Colleges, 26th Edition, Fallbrook, CA: Rugg Publishing.

Steinberg, J. (2002) The Gatekeepers: Inside the Admissions Process of a Premier College, New York, NY: Penguin Books.

Tanabe, G. and K. (2011) The Ultimate Scholarship Book. Belmont, CA: SuperCollege, LLC.

Thacker, L. (2004) College Unranked: Affirming Educational Values in College Admissions, Portland, OR: The Education Conservancy.

Section 2: Writing a "Wow" Application Essay

About Writing in General

Ackerman, A. (2012) The Emotion Thesaurus: A Writer's Guide To Character Expression

Elbow, P. (1998) Writing With Power, New York, NY: Oxford University Press.

Goldberg, N. (2014) The True Secret of Writing, New York, NY: Bantam Books.

Lamott, A. (1995) Bird by Bird, New York, NY: Anchor Books.

Lunsford, A. (2013) EasyWriter, Boston, MA: Bedford /St. Martin's.

Rodale, J. I. (1986) The Synonym Finder, New York, NY: Warner Books.

Strunk, Jr., W. (2000) The Elements of Style, Boston, MA: Allyn and Bacon.

Zinsser, William (2016) On Writing Well, New York, NY: Harper Collins.

About College Essays Or Applying To College

Bauld, H., (2012) On Writing the College Application Essay, New York, NY: Quill.

Berk, N. (2011) College Bound and Gagged: How to Help Your Kid Get into a Great College without Losing Your Savings, Your Relationship, or Your Mind. Pittsburgh, PA: Nancy Berk Media.

Fiske, E. (2014) Real College Essays that Work, Naperville, IL: Sourcebooks.

Merion, D. (September, 2005) "Paper Cut – The U-M Picks Its Freshman Class," *Ann Arbor Observer*. http://www.essaycoaching.com/papercut.pdf

Princeton Review (2014) College Essays That Made a Difference, New York, NY: Princeton Review.

Tanabe, G. and K. (2015) 50 Successful IVY LEAGUE Application Essays. Belmont, CA: SuperCollege, LLC.

Section 3: Scoring Your Best on Those Nerve-Wracking College Admissions Tests

Cracking the ACT with 6 Practice Tests, 2016 Edition. (2015). Natick, MA: The Princeton Review.

Kaplan's New SAT Premier 2016 with 5 Practice Tests: Personalized Feedback + Book + Online + DVD + Mobile. (2015). New York: Kaplan Publishing.

The Official SAT Study Guide. (2016) Reston. VA: College Board.

The Real ACT. (2015) Iowa City, IA: ACT Publications.

ACT: www.act.org

Bizer, L. and G. Markel (2007) Parent's Guide to the SAT & ACT: Practical Advice for You and Your Teen. CD or Download: Ann Arbor, MI: Managing Your Mind, LLC. www.managingyourmind.com.

Burchers, B. and S Burchers, Jr. (2013) Vocabulary Cartoons: Kids Learn a Word a Minute and Never Forget It. Punta Gorda, FL: New Monic Books, Inc.

Dulan, S. (2010) 10 ACT Practice Tests. Second Ed. New York, NY: McGraw-Hill Companies.

Ehrenhaft, G. (2014) Grammar Workbook for the SAT, ACT, and More. Hauppauge, NY: Barron's Educational Series, Inc.

Khashoggi, K., Astuni, A. and K. Kang. (2015) ACT Reading Practice Book (Advanced Practice Series) (Volume 5). Metuchan, NJ: ILEX Publications.

Kravets, M. & Wax, I. (2014) The K & W Guide to Colleges for Students with Learning Differences, 12th Edition. The Princeton Review, New York, NY: Random House.

Lewis, N. (2014) Word Power Made Easy: The Complete Handbook for Building a Superior Vocabulary. New York: Random House LLC ADD

Markel, G. (2012) A Study Tip a Day Gets You an "A": 365 Secrets of Study Success. Ann Arbor, MI: Managing Your Mind, LLC.

Ohayon, M. (2012) The ACT for Bad Test Takers. Louisville, KY: Bad Test Takers.

Stofka, T. (2012) Test Anxiety: Easy Ways to Remove Test Anxiety and Exam Stress (The Test Taker's Guide Series Book 1) Kindle Edition.

APPENDIX I:

Worksheet for Finding the College that Fits

John B. Boshoven, MA., MSW, LPC (boshoven@aaps.k12.mi.us)

The attached worksheet is used during the Junior Conference at Community High School in Ann Arbor.

Students complete the questionnaire with their parents before the conference and counselors use the information to prepare for the conference.

Students are told:

> It's time for your Junior Conference...time devoted exclusively to you and your family. During your Junior Conference, we will concentrate on your plans for the future. We will discuss options available to you and develop a plan or "road map" to help accomplish the goals you've established.

WELCOME to your Junior year! If the last two years went quickly, imagine how fast the next months will fly! It's time to begin the planning of your next steps, what you want to do after high school. Please complete this page and the following pages. Return them to your counselor.

Name _____

Address _____

Telephone _____

Cell Phone _____

E-mail _____

Social Security # (optional) _____

Family Data

Mother: _____

Occupation: _____

Employed: _____

College Attended: _____

Father: _____

Occupation: _____

Employed: _____

College Attended: _____

Siblings: name _____ age_____

                name _____ age_____

                name _____ age_____

                name _____ age_____

Please explain any circumstances regarding your family that I should be aware of. (example: divorced, separated, deceased, illness in family)

_____

_____

All About YOU!

What are you preparing yourself for? (College, Employment, Armed Forces....be specific)

_____

_____

_____

Is your academic record an accurate measure of your ability? Why or Why not?

_____

_____

_____

Describe your academic experience at Community High...What subjects have you enjoyed most?
What subjects least?

_____

_____

_____

_____

What are your academic strong points? What skills do you need to improve?

_____

_____

List 5 words that describe you:

1. _____

2. _____

3. _____

4. _____

5. _____

What books have had an impact on you? What papers or magazine do you regularly read?

_____

_____

_____

What kind of person are you at this point in your life? Be specific: introvert, extrovert, leader, follower Are you a doer or a thinker? Logical or impulsive?

_____

_____

_____

_____

What kind of person would you like to become?

_____

_____

_____

_____

Your Brag Sheet

Academic honors: (list certificates, projects, awards, year received)

_____

_____

_____

Leadership Activities: (state years)

_____

_____

_____

Athletic Participation: (state years)

_____

_____

_____

Volunteer Service:

_____

_____

_____

Employment: (give dates)

_____

_____

_____

Travel Adventures: (countries, summer programs, camps)

_____

_____

_____

Music/Arts Participation

_____

_____

_____

COLLEGE QUESTIONNAIRE

Please complete the following, if you have plans to attend any college.

Do you have a specific location in mind? _____

How far from home would you like to be? _____

Do you prefer a big city? Suburb? Small town? _____

Do you think your parents have a certain location in mind?_____

If you and your parents have conflicting opinions about this, how will it be resolved?

_____

_____

Do you have a specific career goal or major in mind? _____

What other academic areas do you hope to pursue in college? _____

_____

Do you work better when you are challenged with hard classes, or when you are near the top of a less competitive group? _____

How hard do you work in high school?
A - Very hard
B - Hard
C - Somewhat hard
D - Minimally

How hard do you expect to work in college?
A - Very hard
B - Hard
C - Somewhat hard
D - Minimally

What special programs would you like to take advantage of in college? *(study abroad, internships, honors college)*

_____

_____

Is it important to attend a prestigious "big name" institution? _____

How important is it to your parents? _____

Do you prefer:

      A - small college (under 3000)

      B - mid-size college (3000 to 10,000)

      C - large college (10,000 + students)

How good are you at asking for help?_____

Do you prefer an undergraduate institution? _____

Would you consider a single-sex school?_____

Would you consider a religious affiliated school? _____

Is racial/ethnic diversity important to you?_____

Do you prefer a conservative or liberal school? _____

What preferences do your parents have regarding campus atmosphere? _____

Will financial aid be necessary?_____

PARENT EVALUATION

Describe one or two major events that you see as a turning point in your son/daughter's development. Include any family situation, medical history, family trauma, and/or personal achievements that might be helpful.

_____

_____

_____

_____

_____

_____

_____

Has his/her high school experiences been positive? If there have been any painful experiences, please include.

_____

_____

_____

_____

_____

_____

COLLEGE QUESTIONNAIRE

Do you have a specific location in mind? _____

How far from home would you like your son/daughter? _____

Do you prefer a big city? Suburb? Small town? _____

Do you have a certain location in mind?_____

Is there a conflict about location with your son/daughter? _____

Of yes, how will you resolve this? _____

Do YOU have a career goal in mind for your student? _____

How hard does your student apply him/herself? _____

Is he/she ready to accept college responsibilities? _____

Is it important to YOU, he/she attend a prestigious university? _____

Do you prefer small, mid-size, or large college?_____

Do you prefer an undergraduate institution? _____

Would you consider a single-sex school?_____

Would you consider a religious school?_____

Is racial/ethnic diversity important to you? _____

Do you prefer conservative or liberal?_____

Will financial aid be necessary?_____

APPENDIX II:
Worksheet for Writing a "Wow!" Application Essay

Debbie E. Merion, MFA, MSW (debbie@essaycoaching.com)

Pre-Writing an Essay

Start selecting your essay topic by using this worksheet:

1. Fill in the blanks.
2. Pick one of your ideas that you are drawn to.
3. Use that as a writing prompt, write quickly for 10 minutes
4. Read your writing, think about it.
5. Repeat, starting at step 2, as often as needed.

Stir Up Your Thoughts and Emotions

Set the timer for one minute and write the first thing that comes into your head. If you can only write three items instead of five, no problem.

Five ways I'm different from my friends

1
2
3
4
5

Five subjects I could talk about for an hour

1
2
3
4
5

Five reasons my friends, teachers, and coaches respect and value my presence

1
2
3
4
5

Five facts I've learned, or experiences I've had, that have surprised me or changed me, even in a small way

1

2

3

4

5

Five public figures (writers, artists, politicians, etc.) I'd like to meet. Why?

1

2

3

4

5

Five reasons I want to go to FABULOUS U *(What you have to offer the school and what it has to offer you.)*

1

2

3

4

5

Five ideas for each of FABULOUS U's essay questions *(Note: if the college you are applying to takes the Common Application, you can write an essay on the topic of your choice.)*

1

2

3

4

5

Your essay will reveal some of your strongest personal characteristics. Take a few minutes to think about your strengths, then turn to the next page.

Circle Your Five Strongest Qualities:

Action-oriented	Energetic	Masterful	Risk-taker
Aware	Flexible	Motivated	Sensitive
Assertive	Friendly	Open-minded	Strong
Careful	Goal-oriented	Organized	Supportive
Caring	Hardworking	Passionate	Tactful
Competent	Helpful	Persistent	Thorough
Considerate	Honest	Persuasive	Tolerant
Creative	Humorous	Poised	Trustworthy
Curious	Imaginative	Political	Warm
Decisive	Intellectual	Precise	Willing
Dedicated	Intelligent	Quick	Worldly
Determined	Intense	Resilient	*(Add others)*
Diligent	Intuitive	Responsible	_____
Easygoing	Inquisitive	Results-oriented	_____
Efficient	Loyal	Rigid	_____

Describe Two Situations About Two of the Qualities

Very briefly describe a situation that occurred (e.g. helping your grandparents move, tutoring at orchestra camp) in the last six months where you acted out one of your strongest qualities.

_____

_____

Now, can you remember a time when you didn't have one of your strong qualities? Why did you change? How did it happen? How are you different now?

_____

_____

Use One of Your Ideas as a Writing Prompt

Now that you've filled in the blanks, we're going to use one of them to do some initial writing, to stir up your thoughts and memories some more. But we're going to try a new way to write—writing quickly and without self-judgment ("it's great," "it's terrible") so that your words will flow easily onto the page. Here are the rules:

   a. Set a timer for 10 minutes.

   b. Select a topic from your fill-in blanks above that you feel drawn to.

   c. After you start the timer, keep your hand moving and don't cross out.

   d. Don't worry about spelling, punctuation, grammar.

   e. Don't judge what you write. Master writing teacher Natalie Goldberg says, "Feel free to write the worst junk in America."

The writing that you produce from your pre-write will not be your essay. However, it will:

• Guide you in making a choice about your topic.

- Get some words on the page.

- Get you started thinking more about yourself. As you write you will remember more, as writer Joan Didion says:

  "I write entirely to find out what I'm thinking, what I'm looking at, what I see and what it means."

Ready, begin! Use the blank space below and additional pages to stir up your thoughts and memories.

Writing Prompt: _____

APPENDIX III:
Worksheet for Those Nerve-Wracking ACT/SAT Tests

Geraldine Markel, PhD (geri@managingyourmind.com)

Action Plan

It takes more than good intentions to do well on a college admissions test. It takes time, organization, and hard work. In other words, you need to move from talk to action.

A test-prep plan provides the means for converting good intentions into meaningful test preparation. Good preparation results in good scores, but great preparation leads to the best scores possible for you. There is no one best test-prep plan. Review the following eight components and develop your own test-prep strategy:

1) **What do I want? Set a Goal:** Although your short-term goal may be an improved score, your long-term goal is to show what you know when performing under very competitive conditions. Your goal is to feel that your study leads to you to feeling greater control, competence, and confidence. Test taking is a life-long skill. Learning to do well on tests such as the ACT or SAT helps to prepare you for the challenge of taking college-level multiple choice and essay tests. It is risky to set a goal to achieve an ACT score that is hundreds of points higher than a previous score. Discuss with your counselor or tutor a range of realistically possible scores. Is your desired score a dream or a real possibility?

Set Your Goal: _____

_____

_____

2) **What do I need to do? Identify Responsibilities for You and Your Parent:** Since you are the one who is taking the ACT and/or SAT, you will do best if you assume responsibility for the studying. List activities for which you will be responsible. Identify how your parents (or tutor/coach) will help you to implement your plan and improve your skills. This removes many sources of conflict and allows you to focus your effort on studying rather than bickering.

Identify Responsibilities: _____

_____

_____

3) **Where Will I Study Best? Identify Effective Study Conditions:** It is important for you to become aware of the ways in which your surroundings help or hinder your study efforts. Your plan should specify where and with whom you want to study or do practice questions. Will you work with a friend? Do you need a tutor? For many students, the idea of an "electric lockdown" provides the quiet think time needed to learn and review material for the ACT or SAT. This means that for 20-minute periods, you shut off the television, iPod, cell phone, and computer. Seriously reduce the distractions from these technological wonders. If you are an unbeliever, do an experiment. Try doing some problems with loud music and some without. Most often, your speed and accuracy will improve when you remove distractions.

Identify Effective Study Conditions: _____

_____

_____

4) **When and for How Long Will I Study? Set a Schedule:** You have a busy life. Unless you schedule study times, little study occurs. Use a regular calendar that covers the time between the current date and the date of the ACT or SAT. Schedule weekly study sessions for you (and possibly a friend) and for a course or tutor. Registering for a course doesn't take the place of studying and, for example, learning new vocabulary words.

Set a Schedule: _____

_____

_____

5) **How Should I Study? Identify Strategies:** Read the introductory information in the practice books, talk to your teachers, ask your friends, or hire a tutor. You need to know test-taking strategies that help you do your best on the ACT or SAT. For example, the reading sections of these tests require skills that you do not practice in your high school classes. You need someone to show you how best to read and answer the questions.

Identify Strategies: _____

_____

_____

6) Who Can Help? Find Resources: Find out about the resources available in your community. For example, some schools and libraries offer free services. Some tutoring services offer packages for college admissions test preparation that are less expensive than the standard commercial courses. Investigate online programs, since they may be cheaper and possibly, shared by several students.

List Resources: _____

_____

_____

7) Who Can I Study With? Find a Study Buddy: You may be a student who benefits from working with a friend or with a small group. You can take a practice test in one or more areas, such as math or reading. Compare answers and discuss how different students arrived at various answers. Work for 15 to 20 minutes, take a short break, and then resume. You and your friends can act as your own coaches. You practice, review how you did, and identify how you can do better. Have fun together while you're learning.

List a Study Buddy: _____

_____

_____

8) How Much Will it Cost? Set a Budget: Costs are an important consideration. Talk about them with your parents. Discuss the estimated costs of various alternatives. Sometimes it is cheaper to hire a college student as a tutor than to register for a commercial course. How many practice books clutter your friends' closets, half used— or for that matter, never opened? Ask your friends if they know of others who have practice books that you can use.

Set a Budget: _____

_____

_____